OXFORD WORLD'S CLASSICS

DANTON'S DEATH
LEONCE AND LENA
WOYZECK

GEORG BÜCHNER was born in 1813 in Goddelau, in the German Duchy of Hessen-Darmstadt, into a family that had been in the medical profession, on his father's side, since the sixteenth century. In 1831 Büchner enrolled as a medical student in Strasbourg, a city politically radical since the French Revolution, but had to move back to Giessen in Germany two years later, in order to qualify for practice in his home country. The stifling oppression of the German town infuriated him after the liberal atmosphere of Strasbourg, and he founded a Society of Human Rights, which was to arouse the suspicions of the authorities. Although Büchner avoided arrest, other members were tried and imprisoned.

In 1835 *Danton's Death* was published, followed in 1836 by the comedy *Leonce and Lena*, which was entered too late for a competition. In the same year he wrote a study of the nervous system of the barbel fish, on the strength of which he was awarded a doctorate at Zurich University, where he started to lecture.

Woyzeck, composed in late 1836 and early 1837, was not published in the author's lifetime; what remains is incomplete. On 2 February 1837 Büchner, who had never been physically strong, fell ill with typhus and died a few days later, at the age of 23.

Apart from the three plays in this volume, Büchner's major works include a novella, *Lenz* (published 1839), about the schizophrenic poet, and *The Hessian Courier*, a subversive political pamphlet written in 1834.

VICTOR PRICE is Head of the German Language Service at the BBC. He is the author of three novels, *The Death of Achilles*, *The Other Kingdom*, and *Caliban's Wooing*, and of a volume of poetry, *Two Parts Water*.

OXFORD WORLD'S CLASSICS

For over 100 years Oxford World's Classics have brought readers closer to the world's great literature. Now with over 700 titles—from the 4,000-year-old myths of Mesopotamia to the twentieth century's greatest novels—the series makes available lesser-known as well as celebrated writing.

The pocket-sized hardbacks of the early years contained introductions by Virginia Woolf, T. S. Eliot, Graham Greene, and other literary figures which enriched the experience of reading. Today the series is recognized for its fine scholarship and reliability in texts that span world literature, drama and poetry, religion, philosophy and politics. Each edition includes perceptive commentary and essential background information to meet the changing needs of readers.

OXFORD WORLD'S CLASSICS

GEORG BÜCHNER

Danton's Death
Leonce and Lena
Woyzeck

Translated with an Introduction by
VICTOR PRICE

OXFORD
UNIVERSITY PRESS

OXFORD

UNIVERSITY PRESS

Great Clarendon Street, Oxford OX2 6DP

Oxford University Press is a department of the University of Oxford.
It furthers the University's objective of excellence in research, scholarship,
and education by publishing worldwide in

Oxford New York

Athens Auckland Bangkok Bogotá Buenos Aires Calcutta
Cape Town Chennai Dar es Salaam Delhi Florence Hong Kong Istanbul
Karachi Kuala Lumpur Madrid Melbourne Mexico City Mumbai
Nairobi Paris São Paulo Singapore Taipei Tokyo Toronto Warsaw

with associated companies in Berlin Ibadan

Oxford is a registered trade mark of Oxford University Press
in the UK and in certain other countries

Published in the United States
by Oxford University Press Inc., New York

English Translation, Introduction, and Chronology
© Oxford University Press 1971

First published as an Oxford University Press paperback 1971
First published as a World's Classics paperback 1988
Reissued as an Oxford World's Classics paperback 1998
Reissued 2008

British Library Cataloguing in Publication Data

Data available

Library of Congress Cataloging in Publication Data
Büchner, Georg, 1813–1837.
Danton's death, Leonce and Lena, Woyzeck.
(Oxford world's classics)
Translation of: Dantons Tod. Leonce und Lena.
Woyzeck.
Reprint, Originally published: Oxford University
Press, 1971. With new introd.
1. Büchner, Georg, 1813–1837—Translations, English.
I. Price, Victor.   II. Title: Danton's death.
III. Title: Leonce and Lena.   IV. Title: Woyzeck.
[PT1828.B6A27 1988]   832'.7   87–34778

ISBN 978–0–19–954035–8

5

Printed in Great Britain by
Clays Ltd, St Ives plc

CONTENTS

INTRODUCTION

I

When Georg Büchner died at twenty-three, his contemporaries, who knew only a garbled version of *Danton's Death*, mourned him as one who could have become a great scientist; for them, he was a man who had put early turbulence—his revolutionary activities and that rather shocking play—behind him, to do work of brilliant promise in the field of comparative anatomy.

He was born into the medical profession. His father, whose family had been doctors since the sixteenth century, was district physician in Goddelau, in the Grand Duchy of Hesse-Darmstadt, when Georg was born, on 17 October 1813. When he was three the family moved to the capital, Darmstadt, where five other children[1] were born.

Georg had his first instruction at home with his mother, from whom he learnt the Hessian folksongs which give *Woyzeck* its characteristic atmosphere. He then went to a private school, and later to the Ludwig-Georgs-Gymnasium, where a school friend remembered him as looking like 'an old picture of Shakespeare, with the expression of a sterling citizen, vigorous but with charm and high spirits. There was reserve in [his face], and determination, and a sceptical scorn for the trivial and vile. The quivering lips betrayed how often he stood in opposition to the world.'

Hard-working, impatient, reserved, perhaps intellectually arrogant, Büchner preferred science to the classics. But he devoured poetry, especially Shakespeare (in the Schlegel-Tieck translations), Homer, Goethe, the German romantics, and folksongs. He and his classmates used to go out into the beech forest near Darmstadt on summer

[1] Four of them were gifted. Wilhelm, born in 1817, made a fortune as a pharmaceutical chemist by developing an improved method of producing artificial ultramarine, and was later a member of the all-German parliament. Luise, born in 1821, was a writer and an active participant in the struggle for women's rights. Ludwig, born in 1824, who like Georg studied medicine, became a leading materialist philosopher, was Darwin's main advocate in Germany, and wrote an important book, *Kraft und Stoff*. Alexander, born in 1827, was a revolutionary in 1848, emigrated to France, and became professor of literature at Caen.

afternoons and read Shakespeare's plays. He read the philosophers too, and soon came to scorn Hegelian dialectic: 'Everything that is true is reasonable', he said. 'Everything that is reasonable is true.' In religion he was an atheist, in politics a convinced revolutionary.

Büchner loathed the small-souled reaction that had ruled Germany since the defeat of Napoleon. He dreamt of freedom, and he and his friend Minnigerode addressed each other as '*citoyen*'. In a prize-day speech at the Gymnasium he praised the suicide of Cato in high-flown but obviously sincere terms:

The Roman knew only one kind of freedom, freedom under the law, to which he freely submitted himself, recognizing its necessity. Caesar had destroyed this freedom; Cato would have been a slave if he had submitted to the law of despotism. And even though Rome was no longer worthy of freedom, freedom itself was worth Cato's living and dying for it.

His sister Luise remembered Georg's slim figure, his high, domed forehead and chestnut hair, his almost girlish hands, as he stood before the audience of teachers, pupils, and parents. But the physical delicacy hid an iron will and a fiery devotion to the cause of political justice.

At eighteen, in the autumn of 1831, Büchner went to study medicine at Strasbourg. It was a very different city from the one Goethe had known sixty years before; its predominantly German culture had been replaced by a French one, and the Revolution had made it politically radical. The autumn Büchner arrived there was a demonstration in support of the Polish general Ramorino, one of the leaders of the unsuccessful 1830 November rising against the Russians. Even as early as this Büchner's emotional and intellectual involvement with the revolutionary cause was inhibited by a sense of the absurd. He gives a dry, ironic account of the demonstration in a letter, ending with the sentence, 'The comedy is over.'

In Strasbourg he lodged in the house of a liberal clergyman, Johann Jakob Jaegle. Jaegle's daughter Minna, a quiet unassuming girl, nursed Büchner through an illness, and they became engaged. She was three years older than he, and they kept the engagement secret until after he had left Strasbourg.

To practise medicine in his home country, Büchner had to do a year of his three-year medical course at a local university, so in the autumn of 1833 he enrolled at Giessen. After the liberal atmosphere of Strasbourg, the petty oppressions of a German principality were infuriating. 'The political circumstances are enough to drive me mad', he wrote. 'The wretched people patiently pull the cart on which the princes and liberals play their monkey tricks. Every evening I pray for hemp and lanterns.' He organized a Society of Human Rights.

He became ill again, this time with meningitis, but recovered and threw himself into work, toiling at his medical books by day and reading philosophy at night. A fellow-student recalled, almost sixty years later:

Frankly we didn't care for this Georg Büchner. He wore a tall hat, always pushed far back on to his neck, constantly had a distasteful expression like a cat in a thunderstorm, held himself completely apart, had dealings only with a ragged genius fallen on evil days, August Becker (generally referred to as 'red August'). His aloofness was considered arrogance; and as he was evidently involved in political agitation and had once or twice let fall revolutionary remarks, it often happened that on our way home from a tavern of an evening we would stop silently in front of his lodgings and give him an ironic cheer. 'Long live Georg Büchner, preserver of the balance of power in Europe and the man who abolished the slave trade!' Although his still burning lamp proved that he was in, he pretended not to hear the yowling.

'Red August' introduced Büchner to Friedrich Ludwig Weidig, leader of the liberal party in Giessen and publisher of an illegal periodical; he was a man who combined progressive ideas with a curious brand of Christian fundamentalism. For Weidig's press Büchner wrote his first work, *The Hessian Courier*, a polemical pamphlet addressed to the peasants of Hesse-Darmstadt, which begins:

PEACE TO COTTAGES! WAR TO PALACES!

The life of the rich is one long Sunday. They live in fine houses, they wear elegant clothes. They have well-fed faces and speak a language of their own. But the people lie before them like dung on the fields. The peasant walks behind the plough; but the rich man walks behind peasant and plough, driving both him and his oxen, taking the grain and leaving the stubble. The peasant's life is one long working day. Strangers devour the fruit of his fields before his very eyes. His whole body is a sore; his sweat is the salt on the rich man's table. . . .

The tone of *The Hessian Courier* recalls Zola's *J'Accuse*; but in the aptness of its economic argument it is more a forerunner of Marx. Büchner realized that economics was the key factor; the reason the peasants were the strongest party for the *status quo*, he said, was that they feared change would leave them even worse off than before. He set about showing just how oppressed they were, how tiny a proportion of the taxes they paid actually benefited them. But Büchner was a revolutionary out of social indignation and a passionate yearning for justice. It is hard to see him subscribing to any rigid political ideology. Indeed, as his subsequent works were to show, his political convictions were undercut by a sense of the pointlessness of life.

The Hessian Courier was strong meat, even for Weidig, who broke up the text with portentous biblical quotations and toned down its radicalism. The pamphlet was printed in July 1834, but never distributed. On 1 August two of Büchner's friends (one was Minnigerode, who spent three years in prison) were betrayed and arrested while trying to smuggle 150 copies into Giessen from the printing works at Offenbach. Büchner was lucky; there was no evidence to incriminate him. The university authorities searched his room in his absence and confiscated some letters; deciding on a bold course he made a formal complaint to the Commissioner for University Discipline. But he knew his arrest could be only a matter of time.

He returned to Darmstadt in October and continued work under his father's supervision. There, in circumstances of great strain and uncertainty, he composed *Danton's Death* in five weeks early in 1835. He wrote the play in his father's laboratory, hiding the manuscript under medical books when his father came in. His brother Ludwig acted as lookout on the stairs, and there was a ladder behind the house in case Georg had to climb over the garden wall in a hurry. Twice during the period of composition he had to attend hearings as a witness (on one occasion he sent Ludwig). As he said later, 'The Darmstadt police were my muses.'

The ostensible reason for writing the play was money; Büchner knew he would soon have to leave Darmstadt. But it is clear from his letters and the play itself that he simply had to write it. The Giessen experience had been traumatic, all the more so because he must have had doubts, even as he wrote it, of the effectiveness of the *Courier*. 'I have been studying the history of the Revolution,' he wrote to Minna.

I feel as though I had been annihilated by the dreadful fatalism of history. I find a terrible uniformity in human nature, an inexorable force, conferred upon all and none, in human circumstances. The individual: mere foam on the wave, greatness pure chance, the mastery of genius a puppet play, a ridiculous struggle against an iron law to acknowledge which is the highest good, to defeat impossible. I'm no longer in the mood to bow my head to the dress uniforms and street-corner orators of history. I am accustoming my eye to blood.

Büchner sent the finished *Danton* accompanied by a desperate letter to Frankfurt, to the liberal young editor Karl Gutzkow. Gutzkow was impressed and recommended it to the publisher Sauerländer. The play appeared, both in the magazine *Phönix* and in book form, during the summer of 1835. Again Büchner's text was mutilated. Gutzkow cheerfully explained that he had to do it; Sauerländer ('a family man who has begotten seven legitimate children in the bonds of matrimony') would not have accepted the frank sexual references. But Büchner left Darmstadt before he could collect his small payment from the publisher. Getting wind of his impending arrest he borrowed some money from his mother and slipped into France on 9 March 1835, making for Strasbourg and Minna.

His departure for France marks the end of his revolutionary activity though, as his letters attest, his opinions remained unchanged. In Strasbourg, probably in the autumn of 1835, he composed the unfinished prose narrative *Lenz*, whose subject is the developing madness of the *Sturm und Drang* poet J. M. R. Lenz. There can be no doubt that Büchner saw his own mental crisis in that of the gifted, passionate, finally unbalanced Lenz; his fragment, sometimes following an account of the poet's illness left by the Alsatian pastor, J. F. Oberlin, who had looked after him, and sometimes adding personal and highly illuminating passages, is a masterpiece of clinical observation.

In the year he remained in Strasbourg Büchner undertook a staggering amount of work: He learned Italian and English. He read Spinoza and Descartes. He translated two plays by Victor Hugo, *Marie Tudor* and *Lucrèce Borgia*, for Sauerländer. Besides *Lenz*, he wrote *Leonce and Lena*,[1] and may have started *Woyzeck* as well. And he did a piece of brilliant and protracted anatomical research.

---

[1] Büchner intended to enter it in a publisher's competition for the best German comedy, but it reached the judges after the closing date and was returned unread.

In the study of anatomy Büchner found a sense of harmony which he could not find in human life. He was strongly attracted by Goethe's idea of an *Urbild*, or simple basic pattern, repeating itself over and over again in the natural world, and undertook to trace such patterns in an analysis of the nervous system of the barbel, or *cyprinus barbus*, a river fish then common in the Rhine. The work required much use of the microscope—a trial for the short-sighted Büchner—and the preparation of hundreds of specimens. The Société d'Histoire Naturelle at Strasbourg, before whom he gave three lectures on his work in April and May 1836, made him a corresponding member and published his paper—the only work of his, besides *Danton's Death*, to appear in his lifetime.

Büchner sent his treatise on the barbel to Lorenz Oken, the natural philosopher, who was professor at the newly founded University of Zürich. Oken found it so impressive that he recommended Büchner for a doctorate without an oral examination, and he was offered a post as Privatdozent in the University. Büchner was reconciled with his stern but not unkind father; his mother was relieved and jubilant; and he went to Zürich in October 1836 with the prospect of a successful career before him.

For the trial lecture he was required to give, Büchner chose another anatomical subject, the skull nerves of fish. It was a brilliant success, and his appointment as lecturer was confirmed. He had already prepared a course of lectures on the comparative anatomy of fish and amphibians, as well as another on speculative philosophy. One of his students remembered forty years later the scientific clarity, the lack of rhetorical overstatement with which he delivered his anatomical lectures. And as he read and lectured and prepared specimens, he went on with the writing of *Woyzeck* and, perhaps, with a play on the Renaissance dramatist and intriguer, Pietro Aretino.[1]

All this feverish activity was cut short by death. On 20 January 1837 he complained of a cold but said he had recovered. A week later he wrote to Minna, 'I have no desire to die and am as healthy as ever I was.' But he had caught typhus, and was soon gravely ill. Three days before

[1] Some scholars have alleged that Minna Jaegle destroyed the MS. of this play, together with Büchner's diary, just before her own death in 1880. There is no evidence that either manuscript, or for that matter a final draft of *Woyzeck*, ever existed.

his death, after a bout of delirium, he said in a calm, solemn voice: 'We do not have too much pain, we have too little. Because through pain we arrive at God. We are death, dust, ashes. How should we complain?' On 17 February Minna arrived from Strasbourg. On the 19th, Büchner died.

II

Büchner never heard a word of his spoken on stage. We do not even know if he ever visited a theatre, although we feel he must have. He approached the drama from the standpoint of literature and with a single intention: the re-creation of reality. In *Lenz* he makes the distracted poet say, in a rare moment of happiness:

> God Almighty made the world as it ought to be, and we can't cobble up anything better; our sole endeavour should be to try and do something in the same line. In everything I demand life, the possibility of existence; then it's all right. We don't need to ask whether it's beautiful or ugly. The feeling that a created work has life is above both these things and is the only criterion in artistic matters. What's more, we don't often meet it. We find it in Shakespeare, and it speaks to us in its entirety in folksongs, and sometimes in Goethe; all the rest you can throw in the fire.

Büchner was a born dramatist. He has the Shakespearean ear for dialogue and the Shakespearean objectivity: he never judges his characters. He creates striking dramatic pictures. He is a master of language. But his special quality, and that which makes him seem more contemporary than almost anything written today, is his total, uncompromising honesty of emotion and intellect. Reacting strongly against the Schillerian drama, with its high-flown sentiments and rhetoric,[1] Büchner gives us in his plays precisely the reality that Lenz advocates: life raw and unadorned; it required supreme artistry to do so.

Danton's Death has been called, with justification, the best first play in world literature. That so large-scale a play should have been written

---

[1] In a letter of July 1835 he wrote: 'Regarding the so-called idealistic poets, it's my opinion that they've given us nothing but puppets with sky-blue noses and an affectation of pathos, not men of flesh and blood with whose joys and sufferings I can sympathize and whose actions inspire me with horror or admiration. In a word, I think a great deal of Goethe or Shakespeare, but very little of Schiller.'

in five weeks is in itself remarkable; that it was Büchner's very first attempt in the medium makes it even more so.

Of course it is very Shakespearean. Danton resembles Hamlet in his refusal to do anything. The action is presented in the Shakespearean manner, in a series of snapshots, with the background constantly changing. The crowd scenes are full of Shakespearean recollections: II. vi has echoes of the Blackheath scene in *Henry VI, Part 2*, and the rebellious mob in III. x is straight out of *Coriolanus*. (But the fine II. ii owes more to Grabbe's *Napoleon, or the Hundred Days*, which had been published in 1831.) The carters in IV. iv remind one of the porter in *Macbeth*, and the executioners in IV. ix are first cousins to the grave-diggers in *Hamlet*.

Büchner outdoes Shakespeare in reproducing his sources. Perhaps a sixth of the play is taken directly from Thiers or Mignet, or from a historical survey of the years 1789 to 1830, *Unsere Zeit* (Our Time) by Carl Strahlheim, which drew heavily on them. In I. iii, for example, the speech of the citizen of Lyons is from Thiers and almost all of Robespierre's from Strahlheim. Robespierre's other great speech, in II. vii, is from Thiers, as is Danton's speech in his own defence before the Revolutionary Tribunal (III. iv). However, this dependence is more apparent than real; Büchner uses his sources to express an overt philosophical theme, which Shakespeare never does.

Büchner's attitude towards his material is set out in a letter to his parents of July 1835, which was also a spirited defence against the charge of immorality:

In my eyes the dramatic poet is no more than a writer of history, but he stands above the latter in that he re-creates history and instead of giving a bald narration transplants us directly into the life of another age. He gives us characters, not characteristics; human figures, not descriptions. His highest task is to get as close as he can to history as it actually happened. His book has no right to be more moral, or less moral, than history itself. But almighty God didn't make history as reading matter for young ladies, so you mustn't hold it against me if my drama isn't designed for that either. After all I can't make paragons of virtue out of a Danton and the bandits of the revolution! If I wanted to portray their depravity then I had to let them be depraved; if I wanted to portray their atheism then I had to let them speak like atheists. . . . I may be reproached for choosing such material. But that objection has long since been refuted. If it were to be sustained then the greatest masterworks of poetry would have to be rejected. The poet isn't a teacher of morals. He invents and creates characters, he brings the past back to life; and people may learn as much from that as they do from studying history and observing what goes on in life around them. If a man really felt like that he would have to give up the study of history altogether because it tells about immoral events, go down the street blindfold in case he saw something indecent, and cry shame on God for creating a world in which there is so much depravity.

No one could reproach Büchner for not sticking to his programme; in fact he goes beyond it. The remarkable speech he gives to the *grisette* Marion in I. v, is an open plea for sexual liberty, for the 'natural man' which Danton also embodies. But we may feel that Büchner is of the devil's party when he allows Marion the last word: 'Enjoy yourself; that's the best way to pray.'

Danton's Death has often been criticized for its lack of action. The dramatic happenings are concentrated in a few scenes, very fine scenes, too; the rest is talk, discussion, reflection. 'Instead of a drama,' wrote Gutzkow, the play's first critic, 'instead of an action that develops, rises and falls, Büchner gives us the last twitches and rattles in the throat that precede death.' There is no development of character; no one learns anything. At the end a few people have died, that is all. Danton and his friends are, in Büchner's own image, like those dying fish brought to Roman banquet tables to delight the diners with their changing play of colours.

In fact Büchner makes his drama not so much out of Danton as out of death. The play is a set of marvellous variations on the anguish of existence. It keeps on restating in newer, more compelling ways the basic theme that life is atrocious, morality non-existent, action pointless. Death, nothingness, is what Danton craves (and his compulsive sexuality is part of this death-wish); but he reaches the ultimate in existential despair when he realizes that the created thing cannot cease to exist. 'That damned argument: something cannot become nothing, there's the misery. Creation has become so broad, there's no emptiness. Everything is packed and swarming. The void has destroyed itself; creation is its wound.'

This is of course Büchner himself speaking; Danton's panic vision of the world as a wild horse dragging him along on its mad career through space is the author's own, as is the whole philosophic resonance of the character. But from the evidence the historical Danton was very much as Büchner portrays him: an engaging ruffian, dissolute, unscrupulous, and lazy, but good-natured and generous. His Hamlet-like refusal to act in his own defence, his reiteration of 'They'll never dare' are factual; but in the play his motives are invested with the nobility of philosophic despair. Büchner gives his 'unheroic hero' many more contradictions than Shakespeare gave Hamlet: Danton is debauched yet in love with his wife; he is a convinced political moderate, yet too bored to defend his convictions; he is intelligent in thought, but stupid to the point of folly in action; he is indolent but capable of bursts of energy. Early critics found the character unconvincing because of these contradictions, but today we accept them and him without question—contemporary life and letters are full of Danton figures—and only marvel that Büchner could have drawn so modern a hero in 1835.

The play turns on the personal conflict between Danton and Robespierre; the historical struggle was between two political lines, moderation and extremism (which, in the revolutionary context, extremism was bound to win), but Büchner heightens it by adding a clash of personalities. Against Danton the 'natural man', the clear-sighted realist railing at humbug, he places Robespierre, the puritan and the hypocrite. There is a contradiction in Robespierre that Büchner is not quite able to resolve: how can a man who appears so stilted and ridiculous beside Danton sway men so effectively as Büchner shows him doing in I. ii and I. iii? Yet how convincing a character he is in all other respects: the politician's blend of clear-headedness and self-deception is beautifully caught; he half believes his own rhetoric and half disbelieves it. His motives are in a muddle: he mixes up his own sense of inferiority to Danton with political notions which in turn are rationalizations of his own self-disgust and inability to inspire friendship. His killing of Camille from frustrated love is gruesome; so is his perverted comparison of his own agony with that of Christ. Robespierre is at his most dangerous politically when he reflects: 'Sin is in the mind. Whether thought becomes action, whether the body carries it out, is mere chance'—a speech that prefigures Orwell's thought police.

Yet perhaps the most terrifying moment in the play, politically speaking, is Saint-Just's speech in II. vii to the National Convention.

There is no historical basis for this; it is pure invention on Büchner's part, and what a chilling insight it gives into the mind of the political fanatic: the awful farrago of inflated rhetoric, debased logic, and inhumanity is put across with a mad sincerity worthy of Hitler.

Finally, what gives *Danton's Death* its particular bite is the tension between Büchner's honesty as an artist and his political convictions. The play reflects his despairing perception that all human action is futile; and the very class for whom the revolution was made, the proletariat, is depicted as cruel and fickle (not that Büchner condemns it for that; its nature too is determined). In that sense it is an anti-revolutionary work.

The least considerable of Büchner's plays, *Leonce and Lena*, has always puzzled the critics. Its succession of bad puns and unfunny jokes are copied from the romantic plays by Brentano and Tieck which Büchner took as models. There is a 'literary', slightly precious feel about the whole play: the influence of Shakespeare, again, and of Musset, is obvious. Moreover, the moonlit comedy is not wholly compatible with the social criticism. German disunity, the futility of the small principalities, is perhaps too mercilessly attacked.

But if we do not allow ourselves to be misled by the subtitle, 'A Comedy', and think of *Leonce and Lena* as an essentially serious play, we realize that it is in fact *Danton's Death* transplanted to the moonlit Belmont of the final act of *The Merchant of Venice*. It is the satyr play after the tragedy of *Danton*, but the satyrs are chastened by what they have seen.

Leonce is as much a Hamlet figure as Danton; but in him the Dantonesque despair is civilized down to a melancholy sense of absurdity. He is elegant where Danton was elemental, but he is just as valid an expression of Büchner's *Weltanschauung*. The point of attack has shifted from cosmic injustice to the foibles and foolishness of men; the targets are idealistic philosophy (in the person of King Peter), court sycophancy, and the brutalized state of the people (largely caused by mentors like the magistrate and the schoolmaster).

As always with Büchner, the play is intensely contemporary. In none of his works is there a stronger sense of *accidie*; its universe is as absurd as anything in Sartre or Camus. And when Valerio, the Sancho Panza figure, pulls off his series of masks, we see that the twentieth-century problem of identity has been suddenly, unexpectedly raised.

It is a profoundly sad play. We cannot imagine any possible happy ending for Leonce and Lena. The final symbolic gesture is Lena's shake of the head as she leans mutely on Leonce's shoulder. But Büchner, with sure dramatic instinct, adds a virtuoso coda, a fantastic vision of Cockaigne which fulfils the same function as the closing bars of *The Marriage of Figaro*.

Büchner based his last, unfinished play, *Woyzeck*, on the case of an ex-soldier who had killed his mistress, and been publicly executed in Leipzig in 1824. The case had probably been discussed often in the Büchner household, for an account of the murderer's background had appeared in 1825 in a medical journal, Henze's *Zeitschrift für die Staatsarzneikunde*,[1] to which Büchner's father was both subscriber and contributor. One can see the attraction of such material for a writer who had cried in anguish, 'What is it in us that lies, murders, steals?' Here was evidence about murder at least, evidence which chimed in with Büchner's own tragic view of life, for Johann Christian Woyzeck was a victim of fate if ever a man was, stricken down by material need and in thrall to his 'voices'. He was a natural subject both for the poet of *Danton* and the political polemicist of *The Hessian Courier*.

But although in the play the middle classes are pilloried, in the persons of the Doctor and the Captain, *Woyzeck* is not a *pièce à thèse*. In method it is neither slice-of-life naturalism, nor larger-than-life expressionism, though it has been claimed as a forerunner of both. Nor is it an anti-militarist tract, as an East German film tried to make of it. It is something far more complex than any of these, a unique work, organically conceived, which defies any attempt to put it in a category.

In writing it Büchner departed radically from his previously expressed aim of keeping as close to historical truth as possible. He was concerned to write a tragedy, and his achievement was to do so with material which fifty years after his death was still regarded as unsuitable. *Woyzeck* was the first working-class tragedy. Until Büchner wrote it, the 'lower orders' had figured as comic or picaresque relief, as in Ben Jonson or Middleton. In the eighteenth century, with Lillo, Lessing, and Schiller, tragedy had been acclimatized to the middle classes; it took Büchner to root it in the people. It is true that he makes

[1] See Appendix, p. 133.

his working-class principals more attractive then their historical originals: but he never departs from their class reality. And the tragedy is a true one because it is not brought about merely by the social circumstances of the characters. Ordinary human actions set in motion a chain of events whose results are incalculable.

Thanks to Büchner's unique combination of indignation, pity and scientific exactness, his Woyzeck—on the face of it an unlikely hero—is a worthy tragic protagonist. In the first place he is the first clinically observed case of psychosis in literature. His symptoms are depicted with brilliant economy: the hallucinations (patterns in mushrooms, fire in heaven, voices coming from the wall), the disorientation, the swings from mental paralysis to panic action, the incipient paranoia. They mesh in with his poverty and social humiliations (the experiments with the peas) to arouse Aristotelian pity and terror.

The decisive factor in Woyzeck's tragedy is the discrepancy between his intellectual and his affective nature. Intellectually he is a man whose reach exceeds his grasp. He has a pathetic longing to understand life, but is not equipped to do so. His mental ambitions plague him. Yet it is quite clear that he has a better instinctive appreciation of what life is about than, say, the Doctor. He is the 'natural man', indeed he is elemental; but his intellectual puzzlement and his economic dependence have made his natural life—his love of Marie and the child—his sole lifeline. When it breaks he is lost. The voices take control. In a sense he becomes a murderer *malgré lui*; the command has come from outside, making him the first instance in literature of the killer who is also a victim.

Marie too is both agent and victim. Her unfaithfulness precipitates the tragedy, but we cannot really blame her. She is spirited, sensual, and pleasure-loving; it is hardly surprising that she is swept off her feet when an attractive—and normal!—man comes along. (Her beauty incidentally is very cleverly suggested, by the classical method of describing its effect on others.) Yet she is not a tart. She knows perfectly well that she is doing wrong, but is possessed with a sense of fatalism: 'Everything is going to the devil anyway.' Her repentance, when it comes, is beautifully handled, movingly but without sentimentality. Her realization of the significance of her actions long after they have taken place is very true to life, and in a curious way looks forward to Proust's 'intermittences du cœur'.

Besides the two central characters, drawn with remarkable fullness for so short a play, Büchner firmly delineates several others, some in only a couple of lines: the deliberately grotesque Captain and Doctor; the drum major, that force of nature; the sympathetic Andres; the barker and the showman; the apprentices; the Jew; the grandmother; Margret; the idiot. The concision, the almost scientific clarity and concentration, are remarkable. Each brief scene contains the essence of what it wishes to convey; intensity is achieved with the absolute minimum of resources. The play is a series of key dramatic moments, the stations of the cross on Woyzeck's way to catastrophe. The terse dialogue, the haunting fragments of folksongs, give it an overpowering bleakness and poignancy. No one could have predicted such a work in 1837; it is completely outside the *Zeitgeist*, an independent product of genius.

III

Büchner's work remained largely unknown until some forty years after his death. Gutzkow published *Lenz* in 1839 in his magazine *Telegraph für Deutschland*, where most of *Leonce and Lena* had appeared the previous year; the complete *Leonce* was not available until 1850, when Ludwig Büchner published his brother's posthumous writings. *Woyzeck* did not see the light until the complete critical edition of Karl Emil Franzos appeared in 1879. Then, in the mid-1880s, Gerhard Hauptmann lectured on Büchner to the Munich writers' club *Durch*. As he said later, 'Georg Büchner's spirit now lived with us, in us, amongst us.' Indeed it was Munich writers who staged Büchner for the first time—an amateur production of *Leonce and Lena* in 1895. By now the naturalist revival had swept Germany and won sympathy for subjects and attitudes like Büchner's. Frank Wedekind claimed to know 'every word and every letter' that he had written.

Danton's Death was put on by the small Freie Volksbühne in Berlin in 1902. But not until 1910 was it given a full professional performance, in the production by Leopold Jessner at the Thalia theatre, Hamburg. Jessner dispensed with complex sets and worked with light, colour, and movement, concentrating the attention firmly on the actors. *Leonce* was staged in Vienna in the following year; and *Woyzeck* was produced for the first time at the Residenz theatre in Munich in 1913.[1]

Max Reinhardt produced *Danton* in 1916, at the Deutsches Theater, Berlin, using a fixed set consisting of steps and columns, against which individual settings were suggested by curtains and simple properties—a barred window for the prison, a rostrum for the National Convention, and so forth. The scenes emerged from darkness, one after another; often individual speakers were spotlighted. The action was swift; Reinhardt cut a third of the text. The crowd scenes were handled with characteristic vigour, the shouts, songs, and laughter of the mob invading the closing lines of the previous scene. By contrast Reinhardt's *Woyzeck* of 1921 (also at the Deutsches Theater) underplayed the elements of social criticism in the play and concentrated on the human side. Again the use of light was masterly.

Since the Second World War, Büchner's plays have had numerous productions on the German stage. *Woyzeck*, being easier to mount, is given more often than *Danton*, which requires the resources of a large theatre. *Leonce* is less frequently performed, but still reaches the stage fairly regularly.

Alban Berg's opera *Wozzeck*, based on Büchner's play, was first performed in Berlin in December 1925, and has been heard on all the major operatic stages of the world, but only in recent years have the plays themselves gained general currency abroad. *Danton's Death* was produced in French by Jean Vilar at the Théâtre National Populaire, Paris, in 1953, and a version in English was the opening production at the new Lincoln Center theatre in New York in 1965. There were pioneer productions of *Danton* at the Mercury Theatre, London, in 1939, and at the Lyric Theatre, Hammersmith, in 1959, the latter with Patrick Wymark as Danton. *Leonce and Lena* was staged in London as early as 1934 (Fortune Theatre). *Woyzeck*'s British *première* was at the Lyric, Hammersmith in 1948. Since then all three plays have had fairly regular performances in Britain. *Danton's Death* was produced by Jonathan Miller at the National Theatre in 1971, for example; *Woyzeck* has been put on twice at the Edinburgh Festival (1973 and 1981) and

---

[1] The production was meant to take place on 17 October, the centenary of Büchner's birth, but was put off till 8 November to avoid clashing with the centenary of the battle of Leipzig.

Leonce and Lena has been seen at Edinburgh once (1971). Other venues for Büchner productions include the Bristol New Vic, the Lyric Theatre, Belfast and the Glasgow Citizens' Theatre. Both *Danton* and *Woyzeck* have been televised by the BBC (*Danton* twice). But it would be premature to speak of a breakthrough. *Danton's Death* is too costly a proposition for most theatres and *Leonce* remains somewhat obscure. *Woyzeck* on the other hand has made a corner for itself in small theatres and university drama groups. But for most theatre-goers Büchner is a respected name rather than a remembered stage experience.

IV

Translating Büchner is always difficult and sometimes virtually impossible. If one can come close to an acceptable version of *Danton's Death* and *Leonce and Lena*, it is because these two plays are written in standard literary language, for which there is usually an equivalent in English. The images are concrete and pictorial—the fish dying in a blaze of colour, Robespierre's stilts—which is a factor working for the translator; the problem is to reproduce the directness and naturalness of the original. *Danton* has many sustained metaphors, like Saint-Just's sentence of history with its clauses and punctuation marks; these come quite naturally in the language of Shakespeare. So do the rather wearisome sustained puns in *Leonce*, like Valerio's on the word 'come'.

With *Woyzeck* we enter a higher realm of difficulty. In the first place the language is so compressed and precise; and secondly, the play is written largely in Hessian dialect and steeped in the atmosphere of Hessian folk-songs. Standard English cannot cope with this combination. I have tried hard to match Büchner's concision; but what can one do with the dialect? Perhaps the ideal translation would be in dialect too—a latterday Robert Burns might be able to render the toughness and poetic qualities of Büchner's idiom.

VICTOR PRICE

June 1987

A CHRONOLOGY OF GEORG BÜCHNER

1813   17 October.   Georg Büchner born in Goddelau, Hesse-Darmstadt, to Dr Ernst Büchner and Caroline, née Reuss.

1814/15   Congress of Vienna, which re-established the old order in Europe.

1816   The Büchners move to Darmstadt.

1819   Carlsbad Decrees, further restricting freedom of the press and universities.

1825   Büchner enters the Darmstadt *Gymnasium* (grammar school).

1830   July Revolution in France, establishing the bourgeois monarchy of Louis Philippe.

     29 September.   Büchner defends Cato's attitude to suicide in a public speech at the Gymnasium.

1831   9 November.   Büchner enrols as a medical student at Strasbourg university.

     4 December.   Reception of General Ramorino and Polish freedom fighters in Strasbourg.

1833   Secret engagement of Büchner and Minna Jaegle.

     31 October.   Büchner enrols as a student of medicine at Giessen university.

1834   Winter. Büchner becomes acquainted with Friedrich Ludwig Weidig and founds a Society of Human Rights in Giessen.

     April.   Engagement with Minna made public.

     Spring.   Writes the original version of the *Hessian Courier*, which Weidig later alters, toning down some passages and adding Biblical quotations.

     31 July.   The Society is betrayed to the authorities; in spite of Büchner's attempt to warn them, Weidig and others will be arrested. Büchner also plans the release of his friend Minnigerode from the Friedberg fortress; this fails because of Minnigerode's poor health.

1835   January.   Büchner summoned to appear before the investigating judges at Darmstadt; there being no evidence against him, he is released.

     Mid-January to late February.   Composition of *Danton's Death* in Darmstadt.

1 March.   Fearing arrest, Büchner leaves Darmstadt for Strasbourg.

April/May.   Publication of extracts from *Danton's Death* in the magazine *Phönix*.

13 June.   Warrant for Büchner's arrest issued in Darmstadt.

July.   *Danton's Death* published.

Summer/Autumn.   Büchner translates two plays by Victor Hugo, *Lucrèce Borgia* and *Marie Tudor*.

November/December.   Composition of *Lenz*.

1836   Winter.   Büchner writes his *Mémoire sur le système nerveux du barbeau* (a fish). He reads this at three meetings (13 April, 20 April, 4 May) of the *Société d'histoire naturelle de Strasbourg*, which undertakes to print it. Büchner is made a corresponding member of the Société.

April/June.   Büchner writes *Leonce and Lena*, intending to enter it for a competition for the best German comedy announced by the publisher Cotta in February.

July.   *Leonce and Lena* arrives after the deadline and is returned unopened.

September.   Büchner is awarded a doctorate at the university of Zurich on the strength of the *Mémoire*.

18 October.   Moves to Zurich.

November.   Gives a trial lecture (*On Skull Nerves*) in Zurich, then begins a regular course of lectures on the comparative anatomy of fishes and amphibia.

Summer 1836–February 1837.   Probable composition of *Woyzeck*.

1837   2 February.   Büchner falls ill with typhus.

19 February.   Death of Georg Büchner. Minna has arrived in Zurich just in time to see him and be recognised by him.

23 February.   Weidig commits suicide in prison in Darmstadt.

1838   Gutzkow publishes an incomplete version of *Leonce and Lena* in the *Telegraph für Deutschland*.

1839   *Lenz* published in the *Telegraph*.

1850   *Posthumous Works* published by Georg's brother Ludwig Büchner. They do not include *Woyzeck*.

1879   *Collected Works* (ed. Karl Emil Franzos) published. *Woyzeck* appears as *Wozzeck*.

1895   3 May.   First performance of *Leonce and Lena* (Intimes Theater, Munich).

1902   5 January.   First performance of *Danton's Death* (Neue Freie Volksbühne, Berlin).

1913   8 November.   First performance of *Woyzeck* (Residenztheater, Munich).

DANTON'S DEATH
A Drama
[1835]

TRANSLATOR'S NOTE

The action occupies twelve days, 24 March to 5 April 1794. The Terror is at its height. The Jacobin government, led by Maximilien Robespierre, has just warded off a threat from the left; Jacques Hébert and his followers have gone to the scaffold. Now a new threat comes from the right, from Danton and his followers, nicknamed '*les indulgents*'.

Georges Danton had himself created the Terror. In the critical summer of 1793 he had held France together, but the price of national unity was the September massacres of royalist sympathizers, carried out by the Committee of Public Safety, which he himself set up. Now, sick of bloodshed, Danton turns against his creature. The play tells of his half-hearted protest and death.

DRAMATIS PERSONAE

GEORGES DANTON
HÉRAULT-SÉCHELLES
CAMILLE DESMOULINS
PHILIPPEAU
LEGENDRE } Deputies of the National Convention
LACROIX
MERCIER
THOMAS PAINE
FABRE D'EGLANTINE

ROBESPIERRE
COLLOT D'HERBOIS
SAINT-JUST } members of the Committee of Public Safety
BARÈRE
BILLAUD-VARENNES

CHAUMETTE, Procurator of the Paris Commune
DILLON, a general
LAFLOTTE
FOUQUIER-TINVILLE, Public Prosecutor
AMAR
VOULAND } members of the Committee of General Security
HERMAN
DUMAS } presidents of the Revolutionary Tribunal
PARIS, a friend of Danton
SIMON, a stage prompter

JULIE, Danton's wife
LUCILE, Camille Desmoulins's wife
SIMON'S WIFE

MARION
ADELAIDE   } *grisettes*
ROSALIE

Ladies at gaming tables; ladies, gentlemen, young gentleman, and Eugénie walking; citizens, citizen-soldiers, a citizen of Lyons and other deputies; Jacobins, presidents of the Jacobin Club and of the National Convention; turnkeys, hangmen, and carters, men and women of the people, *grisettes*; a ballad-singer, a beggar, a boy, etc.

ACT ONE

Scene I

A drawing room.

HÉRAULT-SÉCHELLES *and some ladies at a card table.* DANTON, *some distance away from them, sitting on a stool at* JULIE's *feet.*

DANTON. Look at the pretty lady. How cunningly she deals her cards. Yes, she really has the knack. They say she always gives her husband a heart and the others—well, her other suits. You women could make us fall in love with a lie.

JULIE. Do you believe in me?

DANTON. I can't tell. We know little of one another. We are pachyderms, we hold out our hands to each other but it's a waste of time. One coarse hide rubs against the other. We are very lonely.

JULIE. You know me, Danton.

DANTON. Yes, as men define knowledge. You have dark eyes and ringlets and a delicate complexion and you call me 'dear George'. But [*touching her forehead and eyes*] there, there, what's behind there? Bah, we have gross senses. Know one another? We would have to break open each other's skulls and squeeze the thoughts out of the brain tissue.

A LADY [*to* HÉRAULT]. What are you doing with your fingers?

HÉRAULT. Nothing.

LADY. Don't crook your thumb like that, it's not decent.

HÉRAULT. But look, the thing has such a suggestive shape.

DANTON. No, Julie, I love you like the grave.

JULIE [*turning away*]. Oh!

DANTON. No, listen. They say there is peace in the grave; the grave and peace are one. If that's so I'm already underground when I lie in your lap. Sweet grave, your lips are passing bells, your voice is my knell, your breast my burial mound and your heart my coffin.

LADY. You've lost!

HÉRAULT. A lover's adventure. It cost money like all the others.

LADY. In that case you declared your love like a deaf-mute, with your fingers.

HÉRAULT. Why not? They say fingers are the easiest things to understand. I got up an affair with a card queen; my fingers were princes turned into spiders; you, madame, were the fairy. But things went wrong. The lady was always in labour; she kept producing knaves. I wouldn't let my daughter play such a game, the kings and queens fall on top of each other so lewdly and the knaves follow close behind.

[*Enter* CAMILLE DESMOULINS *and* PHILIPPEAU.]

HÉRAULT. Philippeau, what glum eyes! Did you tear your red cap? Did Saint Jacques snarl at you? Did it rain at the executions? Or did you have a bad seat and see nothing?

CAMILLE. You're parodying Socrates. Do you remember what the divine old buffer said to Alcibiades when he found him moody and depressed? 'Did you lose your shield on the battlefield? Were you beaten in the footrace or the fencing? Did someone sing or play better than you?' These classical republicans! Take some of our guillotine romanticism as an antidote.

PHILIPPEAU. Twenty victims today. We were wrong. The Hébertistes went to the scaffold for one reason only: they weren't systematic enough. Or perhaps the Decemvirs[1] realized they were lost if for a single week there existed men more feared than themselves.

HÉRAULT. They would like to bring back the Stone Age. Saint-Just would be delighted if we crawled around on all fours so that the lawyer from Arras[2] could rig us up with dunces' caps, school-benches, and a mechanical God Almighty, supplied by the Geneva watchmaker.[3]

PHILIPPEAU. They wouldn't mind adding a couple of noughts to Marat's proscription figures either. How much longer must we crawl in slime and blood like new-born infants? How much longer

---

[1] The Committee of Public Safety. The men of the revolution affected the ancient Roman style.

[2] Robespierre.   [3] Jean-Jacques Rousseau.

have coffins as cradles and play ball with human heads? We must go forward. The Committee of Clemency must be implemented, the expelled deputies must be reinstated!

HÉRAULT. The revolution has entered the period of reorganization. We must call a halt to revolution, and start the republic! In our constitution right must replace duty, happiness virtue, and protection punishment. Every individual must carry weight; every individual must be free to assert his nature. Whether he's reasonable or unreasonable, educated or uneducated, good or bad, is no concern of the state. We are all fools and no one has the right to impose his particular brand of folly on anyone else. Everyone must be able to enjoy himself in his own way—but not at others' expense, not if he interferes with other people's enjoyment.

CAMILLE. The constitution must be a transparent garment clinging to the body politic. It must register the impress of every artery-pulse, every flexed muscle, every tautening of a ligament. Let the body be beautiful or hideous as it chooses; it has that right. We are not entitled to cut it a coat to our measure. These people are trying to throw a nun's veil over the bare shoulders of this lovely, sinful France of ours, but we will rap them on the knuckles! We want naked gods, Bacchic women, Olympic games, and from tuneful lips oh, such songs of cruel, limb-slackening love! We don't want to stop the Romans sitting in the corner boiling turnips, but they mustn't keep ramming these gladiatorial games down our throats. Divine Epicurus and sweet-buttocked Venus—these must be the doorkeepers of the republic, not Saints Marat and Chalier.[1] Danton, you shall lead the offensive in the Convention!

DANTON. I shall, thou wilt, he will . . . If only we live to see the day, as old women say. In an hour's time another sixty minutes will have passed. Isn't that so, my boy?

CAMILLE. What's your drift? That's obvious.

DANTON. Everything is obvious. Only who's to bring all these pretty things to pass?

PHILIPPEAU. We and all honest men.

---

[1] Jacobin martyrs. Marat was murdered in his bath by Charlotte Corday; Chalier was killed in Lyons by anti-Jacobin forces.

DANTON. That 'and' is a long word. It puts too much distance between them and us. Honesty will be out of breath by the time we get together. And even if not—you can lend money to an honest man, stand godfather to his children, marry your daughter to him; but that's the limit.

CAMILLE. If that's how you feel why did you start the fight in the first place?

DANTON. I couldn't abide those people. I never could look at strutting Catos of that sort without giving them a kick. It's just my nature.
[*Stands up.*]

JULIE. You're not going?

DANTON [*to* JULIE]. I must. They're badgering me again with their politics. [*As he goes out*] Between the door and the doorpost I will prophesy unto you: the statue of liberty has not yet been cast. The furnace is red-hot. We may yet burn our fingers.   [*Exit.*]

CAMILLE. Let him go. Do you think he can keep his hands off when it comes to action?

HÉRAULT. That's true. But only to kill time, like playing chess.

SCENE II

A street.

SIMON, *his* WIFE.

SIMON [*beating his* WIFE]. You brothel-madam, you wizened old pox-pill, you maggotty Eve's apple!

WIFE. Help, help!

[*Crowd comes running.*]

CITIZENS. Pull them apart, pull them apart!

SIMON. Unhand me, Romans! I'll rip this carcass asunder. You vestal virgin!

WIFE. Me, a vestal? I'd like to see the day!

SIMON.   'Thus from thy shoulders do I tear the robe
                And fling thy carrion naked in the sun!'
You whore's groundsheet, every wrinkle of your body harbours
lust!   [*Crowd separates them.*]

1 CITIZEN. What's up?

SIMON. Where's the virgin? Speak! No, no, I can't call her that. The
maiden. No, not even that. The woman, the wife. Not even that.
Only one other name exists, and oh, it chokes me! I haven't the
breath for it.

2 CITIZEN. And a good job, too, otherwise it would stink of brandy.

SIMON. Old Virginius, cover your ungarnished head. The raven of
shame sits upon it, pecking at your eyes. A knife, Romans, give me a
knife!

WIFE. He's a good-hearted man, but he can't hold his liquor. The brandy
trips him up.

2 CITIZEN. It puts a third foot under him.

WIFE. It trips him up, I tell you.

2 CITIZEN. Exactly. *First* it gives him three feet, then he trips on the
third, and then the third falls too.

SIMON. Vampire, bloodsucker, you've had my heart's blood!

WIFE. Just leave him alone: it's his time for snivelling now. You'll see.

1 CITIZEN. What's the trouble anyway?

WIFE. It was like this. I was sitting there on a stone, warming myself in
the sun—because we've got no firewood . . .

2 CITIZEN. Try your husband's nose, if you want kindling!

WIFE. And my daughter had just gone off to do her stint on the corner—
she's a good girl and supports her parents.

SIMON. She admits it!

WIFE. You Judas! Would you have breeches to pull up if the young
gentlemen didn't pull down theirs? You brandy cask, you'll thirst
if her well runs dry. Do you want that? We work with the whole
of our body—let her work with the hole of hers. Her mother did

yeoman service with it to bring her into the world, and by God it hurt. Why shouldn't she pay her back? You don't think it hurts *that* way, do you, you donkey?

SIMON. Ah, Lucretia! A knife, Romans, give me a knife! Oh, Appius Claudius!

1 CITIZEN. Yes, a knife, but not for the poor tart. What did she ever do? It's her hunger that's the whore and beggar. A knife for the men who buy the flesh of our wives and daughters. Woe to those who whore-monger with the daughters of the people! Your bellies are full of wind, they groan with indigestion. Your jackets are in tatters; they have warm overcoats. You have welts on your fists, their hands are like velvet. *Ergo*, you toil and they do nothing. *Ergo*, you earn a living, and they steal it from you. *Ergo*, if you want to get back a groat's worth of your filched property you must go whoring and begging. *Ergo*, they are villains and you must put them to death.

2 CITIZEN. They have no blood in their veins but what they've sucked from ours. They told us: Kill the aristos, they are wolves. So we strung up the aristos. They told us: The veto[1] is taking the bread from your mouths. So we killed the veto. They told us: The Girondins are starving you. So we guillotined the Girondins. But they pulled the clothes from the dead men's backs and left us freezing and barefoot as before. Well, we'll flay the hide from their legs and make trousers from it; we'll melt down their fat to thicken our soup. Death to anyone without a hole in his coat!

1 CITIZEN. Death to anyone who can read and write!

2 CITIZEN. Death to anyone who walks with his toes turned out!

ALL. Death, death!

[*A* YOUNG MAN *is dragged in.*]

VOICES. He has a handkerchief. An aristo! To the lantern with him!

2 CITIZEN. What, he doesn't blow his nose with his fingers? String him up!

YOUNG MAN. Messieurs. . . .

2 CITIZEN. There are no messieurs here! Up with him!

---

[1] The King. So called by the revolutionaries because he had the right of veto in the National Assembly under the constitution of 1791.

SOME CITIZENS [*sing*].

> The worms crawl in, the worms crawl out,
> They crawl in thin and they crawl out stout—
> Better to hang in the light of day
> Than let them gnaw your bones away.

YOUNG MAN. Mercy!

3 CITIZEN. Just one little game with a hempen necktie! It'll only take a moment. We're more merciful than you. Our whole life is murder by hard labour. We dangle from a rope for sixty years, and we dance! Well, now we're going to cut ourselves down. To the lantern with him!

YOUNG MAN. Get on with it then. You won't see any the better for it.

CROWD. Bravo, well said!

A FEW VOICES. Let him go!   [YOUNG MAN *runs away.*]

[*Enter* ROBESPIERRE, *accompanied by sans-culottes and women.*]

ROBESPIERRE. Citizens, what's the trouble?

3 CITIZEN. What do you think! The few drops of blood spilled in August and September haven't put any red in our cheeks. The guillotine is too slow. We need a cloudburst.

1 CITIZEN. Our wives and children are crying for bread, and we're going to feed them with the flesh of the aristos. Death to anyone with a whole coat!

ALL. Death, death!

ROBESPIERRE. In the name of the law!

1 CITIZEN. What is the law?

ROBESPIERRE. The will of the people.

1 CITIZEN. Well, we're the people. And our will is that there shouldn't be any law. *Ergo*, our will is law, *ergo*, in the name of the law there is no law. *Ergo*, death!

VOICES. Silence for Aristides! Silence for the Incorruptible!

A WOMAN. Silence for the Messiah who is sent to elect and to judge. He will give the wicked to the edge of the sword. His eyes are the eyes of election, his hands the hands of judgement.

ROBESPIERRE. Poor virtuous people. You do your duty, you offer up your enemies. People, you are great! In lightning flashes and the roll of thunder you stand revealed. But, people of France, your blows must not injure your own body; you are mangling yourself in your rage. You can be brought low only through your own strength; your enemies know that. Your legislators are watchful, they will guide your hands. Their eyes are unblinking, and your hands are inexorable. Come with me to the Jacobins! Your brothers will open their arms to you, and we will hold a bloody tribunal on our enemies.

MANY VOICES. To the Jacobins, to the Jacobins! Long live Robespierre.
[*All exeunt.*]

SIMON. Alas, they've abandoned me.   [*Tries to get up.*]

WIFE. There.   [*Supports him.*]

SIMON. Ah, my Baucis! You heap coals of fire on my head.

WIFE. Now stand up.

SIMON. You're turning away? Can you ever forgive me, Portia? Did I strike you? Not my hand, not my arm did it, but my madness.
      'His madness is poor Hamlet's enemy.
      Then Hamlet did it not, Hamlet denies it.'
   Where's our daughter, where's our little Suzon?

WIFE. There, on the street corner.

SIMON. Let's go to her. Come, virtuous spouse!   [*Exeunt.*]

SCENE III
The Jacobin Club.

[ROBESPIERRE, LEGENDRE, COLLOT D'HERBOIS, JACOBINS.]

A CITIZEN OF LYONS. Our brothers from Lyons have sent us to pour the gall of their anger into your breasts. We do not know whether the tumbril that carried Ronsin[1] to the guillotine was the hearse of liberty. But we do know that since that day the murderers of Chalier have walked the earth as solidly as if there was no such thing as a grave for

---

[1] Hébertiste leader, executed 24 March 1794.

them. Have you forgotten that Lyons is a stain on the soil of France that must be covered with the bones of traitors? Have you forgotten that this harlot of the monarchies has only the waters of the Rhône to wash clean her sores? Have you forgotten that the revolutionary tide must run Pitt's battle fleets aground on the corpses of the nobility? You are murdering the revolution with your compassion. The breath of a single aristocrat is the death-rattle of freedom. Only cowards die for the republic; Jacobins kill for her. I tell you this: if we no longer find in you the vigour of the men of the 10th of August, of September, of the 31st of May, our only resource is, as it was for the patriot Gaillard, the dagger of Cato.

[*Applause and confused shouting.*]

A JACOBIN. We will drink the cup of Socrates with you!

LEGENDRE [*forces his way to the tribune*]. We have no need to look as far as Lyons. There are those here who wear silk clothes, drive around in carriages, sit in boxes at the theatre, and talk like the dictionary of the Academy. Their heads have been firm on their shoulders these last days. They are great wits—they say we must give Marat and Chalier a double martyrdom and guillotine them in effigy.

[*Violent reactions in the assembly.*]

VOICES. They are dead men. Their tongues have guillotined them!

LEGENDRE. The blood of these saints be upon them! I ask the members of the Committee of Public Safety here present, since when have they been so hard of hearing . . .

COLLOT D'HERBOIS [*interrupting him*]. And I ask you, Legendre, whose voice breathes life into such thoughts, who gives them the boldness to speak? It's time to tear off the mask. Listen to me! The cause is denouncing its effect, the cry its echo, the act its consequence. The Committee of Public Safety understands logic better than that, Legendre. Be calm! The busts of our two saints will remain undisturbed. Like Medusa-heads they will turn the traitors to stone.

ROBESPIERRE. I demand the right to speak.

THE JACOBINS. Silence. Silence for the Incorruptible!

ROBESPIERRE. This cry of exasperation from all sides was what we were waiting for. Now we will speak. Our eyes were open, we saw the enemy start up in arms, but we did not sound the alarm. We let the people look to their own defence, and they have not slumbered.

They have taken up arms. We let the enemy sally forth from his ambush. Now he stands free and unconcealed in the light of day. Every blow will strike home; the moment you see him, he is a dead man.—I have told you before this: the internal enemies of the republic have split into two factions, like two armies. They fight under different colours, and they follow different paths. But their goal is the same. One of these factions is no more. In its madness and affectation it sought to discredit the most seasoned patriots as worn-out weaklings, in order to rob the republic of its most powerful arms. It declared war on God and on property to create a diversion in favour of the monarchies. It parodied the sublime drama of the revolution to compromise it by studied excesses. The triumph of Hébert would have thrown the republic into chaos and despotism would have been satisfied. The sword of the law has struck down the traitor. But what do the foreigners care while criminals of another sort remain to achieve the same end? We have done nothing so long as another faction remains to be destroyed. This faction is the mirror-image of the first. It incites us to be weak, its battle cry is mercy. It wishes to deprive the people of their weapons and the strength to use them, in order to hand them over naked and enfeebled to the monarchs. The weapon of the republic is the Terror, the strength of the republic is virtue—virtue because without it terror is corruptible, and terror because without it virtue is powerless. The Terror is an emanation of virtue; it is no more than swift, stern, inexorable justice. They say terror is the weapon of despotism, so our government resembles a despotism. Of course it does! But only as the liberator's sword resembles the sabre of a tyrant's lackey. If a despot rules his brutish subjects through terror, he is justified as a despot. If you as founding fathers of the republic use terror to smash the enemies of liberty, you are no less justified. The revolutionary government is the despotism of freedom against tyranny. Mercy for the royalists, cry some. Mercy for scoundrels? No! Mercy for the innocent, mercy for the weak, mercy for the unfortunate, mercy for mankind! Only the peace-loving citizen can claim protection from society. In a republic only republicans are citizens; royalists and foreigners are enemies. To punish the oppressors of mankind is mercy; to pardon them is barbarism. Every show of false sentiment is in my opinion a sigh that flies to England or to Austria. But not content with disarming the people, this faction is trying to poison the holiest sources of their strength with vice. This is the subtlest, most dangerous, and most hateful way of attacking freedom. Vice is the distinguishing sign of aristocracy, its mark of Cain. In a republic it is not only a moral but also a political crime. Libertinism is the political enemy of liberty; the greater the apparent services of the libertine the more dangerous he is. The most dangerous citizen of all is one who wears out a dozen red bonnets before he can bring himself to perform a single virtuous action. You will not fail to understand me, if you think of those who once lived in garrets and now ride in carriages and commit fornication with ci-devant *marquises* and *baronnes*. We may well ask, 'Have they robbed the people? Or have they taken a golden handshake from the kings?' when we see these lawgivers of the people flaunting every vice and luxury of the former courtiers, when we see these counts and marquesses of the revolution marrying rich wives, giving sumptuous banquets, gambling, keeping servants, and wearing costly clothes. We may well stand astonished when we hear them delivering *bons mots*, parading their wit and laying claim to good taste. We have just listened to a shameless parody of Tacitus. I could answer out of Sallust and travesty Catiline. But no further brush-strokes are necessary, I think. Their portraits are complete. No accommodation, no truce with men whose only thought has been to plunder the people and whose hope was to carry out their extortions with impunity, men for whom the republic has been speculation and the revolution trade! Terrified by the rising tide of examples, they are trying ever so gently to dampen the ardour of justice. It is as if they said to themselves: 'We are not virtuous enough to wield such terror. You philosophic lawgivers, pity our weakness. I dare not admit that I am vicious, so I implore you rather to be merciful!' Be cool, virtuous people. Be calm, patriots. Tell your brothers in Lyons: the sword of the law is not rusting in the hands to which you have entrusted it. We shall set the republic a great example.

[*General applause.*]

MANY VOICES. Long live the republic, long live Robespierre!

PRESIDENT. The session is closed.

SCENE IV
A street.

LACROIX, LEGENDRE.

LACROIX. What have you done, Legendre? Do you realize whose heads you're knocking down with those busts of yours?

LEGENDRE. A few dandies and elegant women, that's all.

LACROIX. You're a suicide, a shadow murdering the man who cast it and itself into the bargain.

LEGENDRE. I don't understand.

LACROIX. I thought Collot spoke plainly enough.

LEGENDRE. What does that matter? The man was drunk again.

LACROIX. Out of the mouths of babes, fools, and—why not?— drunkards . . . Whom do you think Robespierre meant by Catiline?

LEGENDRE. Well, whom?

LACROIX. It's simple. The atheists and ultras have been packed off to the scaffold. And much good it has done the people—they're still running the streets barefoot, howling for the skin of the aristos to make boots with. The temperature of the guillotine mustn't fall. A couple of degrees lower and the Committee of Public Safety may as well bunk down in the Place de la Révolution.

LEGENDRE. What have my busts got to do with that?

LACROIX. Can't you see? You've officially proclaimed the fact of counter-revolution. You've forced the Decemvirs to act, you've guided their hand! The people are a minotaur. They have to have their weekly dole of corpses, otherwise they'll eat *them*.

LEGENDRE. Where's Danton?

LACROIX. How should I know? He's hunting down the Medici Venus piecemeal in all the *grisettes* of the Palais Royal. He calls it playing mosaics. Heaven knows which limb he's got to by now. It's a shame that nature hacks up beauty like Medea her brothers and buries the fragments in so many bodies.—Let's go to the Palais Royal.

SCENE V

A room.

DANTON, MARION.

MARION. No, don't touch me! Not while I'm at your feet like this. I want to tell you a story.

DANTON. You could put your lips to better use.

MARION. No, leave me alone for once. My mother was a clever woman; she used to tell me that chastity was a great virtue. When people came to the house and started talking about you-know-what she sent me out of the room. If I asked what they meant she said, 'Shame on you'. If she gave me a book there were nearly always a few pages for me to skip. But I could read what I liked of the Bible: it was holy writ. There were things in it I couldn't understand. I didn't like asking anybody, so I thought them over for myself. Then the spring came; something was happening all round me, and I had no part in it. I got into an odd state. I felt . . . stifled, almost. I looked at my own limbs. Sometimes I felt as if I were two separate people, then the two melted into one again. About that time a young fellow used to come to our house. A good-looking lad; he used to say silly things about me. I didn't rightly know what he meant but I had to laugh. My mother invited him quite often. That suited us both very well. We were allowed to sit together. Finally we thought: why not swop our chairs for a pair of sheets? I enjoyed that more than listening to his chat. We did it on the sly, but I didn't see why I should be allowed the small pleasure and denied the big one. And so it went on. But I was a sea, and the depths of me had been stirred; I swallowed up everything. For me every partner was the same; all men merged into a single body. Well, it's the way God made me; nobody can get out of that. In the end the boy noticed. One morning he came and kissed me as if he were going to throttle me. He wound his arms round my neck; I was petrified. Then he let me go and laughed and said he had almost done something stupid. He said, 'Keep your poor rags of flesh; they're all you've got. Put them to work. They'll soon wear out anyway.' He said he wouldn't spoil my fun prematurely. Then he went away. I didn't know what he meant. That evening I was sitting at my window, I was just sort of floating away on the waves of the sunset (I'm very sensitive, you know; I only know what's going on through my nerves). Then a crowd came down the street, with children running in front and women gaping out of windows. I looked down and it was him. They carried him past in a laundry basket. The moon shone on his pale forehead, and his hair was wet. He had drowned himself. I couldn't help crying. That was the one big gap in my life. Other people have Sundays and week-days, they work six days and they pray on the seventh. Every year they look forward to their birthday, and to the New Year, and they feel sentimental. I don't understand all that. I know nothing about divisions or changes. I'm all of a piece, just one big longing and clinging. I'm a fire, a river. My mother died of grief. People point their fingers at me. That's stupid! The only thing that counts is what you enjoy—bodies, holy pictures, flowers, toys. The feelings are just the same. Enjoy yourself—that's the best way to pray.

DANTON. Why can't I take your beauty into myself? Why can't I embrace it completely?

MARION. Danton, your lips have eyes.

DANTON. I wish I were part of the air, to flood round you and break on every wave of your lovely body.

[*Enter* LACROIX, ADELAIDE, ROSALIE.]

LACROIX [*standing in the doorway*]. I really can't help laughing!

DANTON [*crossly*]. What is it?

LACROIX. I was thinking about the street.

DANTON. Well?

LACROIX. There were a couple of dogs out there—a mastiff and a Maltese spaniel. They were trying to mount each other.

DANTON. What about it?

LACROIX. I just happened to think of it and it made me laugh. It was an edifying sight! The girls were looking out the windows. We ought to know better than to let them sit in the sun. Flies couple on their hands and put ideas in their heads. Legendre and I have been in nearly every cell here, the Little Sisters of the Revelation—Carnal, not Carmel—hung on to our coattails demanding a blessing. Legendre's with one of them now, mortifying her flesh, but he'll get a month's penance out of it himself. I've brought along these two priestesses with the divine Host.

MARION. *Bonjour*, Mademoiselle Adelaide. *Bonjour*, Mademoiselle Rosalie.

ROSALIE. It's a long time since we had the pleasure.

MARION. I've been sorry not to see you.

ADELAIDE. God, but we were busy. Day and night.

DANTON [*to* ROSALIE]. How supple your hips have got, my dear.

ROSALIE. Getting better every day, I am.

LACROIX. What's the difference between an ancient and a modern Adonis?

DANTON. And Adelaide has got morally ambiguous. A very piquant variation: she wears her face like a fig leaf for her body. Such a fig tree on so well-travelled a road—a refreshing shade indeed!

ADELAIDE. I'd be a cattle-track if monsieur had his way. . . .

DANTON. *Touché*! But don't be cross, mademoiselle.

LACROIX. Listen, will you? Your modern Adonis is torn not by a boar but by sows. He gets his wound not in the thigh but in the privates. His blood crystallizes not into rosebuds but into flowers of mercury.[1]

DANTON. Mademoiselle Rosalie is a restored torso of which only the legs and hips are authentic. She's a compass needle. What her north pole repels her south pole attracts. Her midriff is an equator, and everyone crossing the line gets ducked in chloride of mercury.

LACROIX. Two Sisters of Mercy, each working in a hospital, the hospital being her own body.

ROSALIE. Shame on you, our ears are burning!

[*Exeunt* ADELAIDE *and* ROSALIE.]

DANTON. Good night, pretty children.

LACROIX. Good night, mines of mercury.

DANTON. They haven't earned their suppers. I'm sorry for them.

LACROIX. Listen, Danton. I've just come from the Jacobins.

DANTON. Any news?

[1] Chloride of mercury was the usual treatment for venereal disease at the time.

LACROIX. The Lyons people read out a proclamation. They said there was nothing left for them but to wrap themselves in their togas. They all pulled faces as if to say to each other: 'It won't hurt, Paetus.' Legendre shouted that some people wanted to smash the busts of Chalier and Marat. I think he's trying to paint his face red again. He's come through the Terror in one piece and the children snatch at his coat in the street.

DANTON. And Robespierre?

LACROIX. Drummed his fingers on the rostrum and said virtue must rule through the Terror. The phrase gave me a pain in the neck.

DANTON. It saws wood for the guillotine.

LACROIX. And Collot yelled like a man possessed that the masks would have to be torn off.

DANTON. The faces will come away with them.

[*Enter* PARIS.]

LACROIX. What's doing, Fabricius?

PARIS. From the Jacobins I went straight to Robespierre. I demanded an explanation. He tried to look like Brutus offering up his sons, spouted generalities about duty and said that where liberty was concerned he was no respecter of persons but would sacrifice everybody—himself, his brother, his friends.

DANTON. That was plain enough. Reverse the order and he's at the bottom of the ladder, helping his friends up to the scaffold. We owe Legendre a debt of thanks: he's made them speak out.

LACROIX. The Hébertistes aren't dead yet, and the people are famished. That's a powerful lever. The weight of blood in the balance daren't lessen or the pan will rise and carry the Committee of Public Safety with it—kicking their heels. The scales need ballast; one heavy head will do the job.

DANTON. I know, I know. The revolution is like Saturn, it eats its children. [*After a moment's reflection*] But they'll never dare.

LACROIX. Danton, you're a dead saint. But the revolution doesn't want to know about relics. It threw the kings' bones in the gutter and heaved the holy statues out of the church door. Do you think they'd leave your monument standing?

DANTON. But my name! The people!

LACROIX. Your name! You're a moderate, and so am I. So are Camille, Philippeau, Hérault. To the people moderation is the same thing as weakness; they cut down the stragglers. The tailors of the Bonnet Rouge section would feel the whole force of Roman history in their needles if the man of September turned out to be more moderate than they.

DANTON. That's true. Besides, the people are children. They have to smash things to see what's inside.

LACROIX. Besides, my dear Danton, we *are* vicious, as Robespierre said. That is to say, we enjoy life. While the people are virtuous—that is, they don't enjoy it. Hard work blunts their senses; they can't get drunk because they haven't got the money; and they can't go to the whorehouse because their breath stinks of cheese and herrings, and that disgusts the girls.

DANTON. They hate libertines as eunuchs hate whole men.

LACROIX. They call us scoundrels, and . . . [*in* DANTON's *ear*] *entre nous* there's some truth in what they say! Can't you see it? Robespierre and the mob will practise virtue. Saint-Just will write a report—in three volumes—and Barère will run up one of his blood-boltered speeches to wrap the Convention in. Oh, I can see it all.

DANTON. You're dreaming. They never had guts without me, and they won't have any against me. The revolution's not over yet. They might still need me. I'm their big gun—they'll keep me in reserve.

LACROIX. We must act.

DANTON. Ways will be found.

LACROIX. They'll be found all right. After we're lost.

MARION [*to* DANTON]. Your lips have gone cold. Words have smothered your kisses.

DANTON [*to* MARION]. So much time to get through! It was worth it. [*To* LACROIX] I'll go to Robespierre tomorrow. I'll anger him and then he'll come out with it. Till tomorrow then. Good night, *mes amis*, good night. And thank you!

LACROIX. My good friends, clear out. Good night, Danton. This girl's thighs will guillotine you: her mound of Venus will be your Tarpeian rock.

[*Exit with* PARIS.]

SCENE VI
A room.

ROBESPIERRE, DANTON, PARIS.

ROBESPIERRE. I tell you, whoever holds my arm back when I draw the sword is my enemy. His motives are beside the point. He who hinders me in my self-defence kills me, as surely as if he had attacked himself.

DANTON. Where self-defence ends murder begins. I see no necessity for going on with these killings.

ROBESPIERRE. The social revolution is not yet accomplished. To carry out a revolution by halves is to dig your own grave. The society of the privileged is not yet dead. The robust strength of the people must replace this utterly effete class. Vice must be punished, virtue must rule through the Terror.

DANTON. I don't understand the word 'punished'. You and your virtue, Robespierre! You've taken no money, you've run up no debts, you've slept with no women, you've always worn a decent coat and never got drunk. Robespierre, you are infuriatingly righteous. I would be ashamed to wander between heaven and earth for thirty years with such a priggish face, for the miserable pleasure of finding others less virtuous than myself. Is there no small, secret voice in you whispering just occasionally: 'You are a fraud'?

ROBESPIERRE. My conscience is clear.

DANTON. Conscience is a mirror before which a monkey pinches itself. Everyone rigs himself up in what finery he has and goes out to have fun in his own way. Why get into each other's hair about it? We all try to defend ourselves against spoilsports. You aim to turn the guillotine into a washtub for other people's stained linen, to use human heads as soap-cakes for dirty clothes—now have you any right to do that just because your own coat is brushed and clean? You're perfectly entitled to hit out if people spit on it or tear holes in it. But what business is it of yours if they leave you in peace? Why should you lock them up in a coffin so long as they don't get in your way? Are you God's policeman? And if the sight's too much for you, as it seems to be for your blessed Almighty, then put a handkerchief over your eyes.

ROBESPIERRE. You deny the existence of virtue?

DANTON. And of vice. There are only Epicureans, coarse ones and fine ones. Christ was the finest. That's the only difference between men that I've been able to discover. Everyone acts according to his nature—in other words he does what does him good. But it's cruel to kick your stilts from under you like this, eh, Incorruptible?

ROBESPIERRE. Danton, there are periods when vice is high treason.

DANTON. For God's sake don't proscribe it. That would be ungrateful. You owe it too much—by contrast, I mean. But to use your own terminology, our blows must be of service to the republic. We mustn't strike the innocent along with the guilty.

ROBESPIERRE. Who says that a single innocent man has suffered?

DANTON. Did you hear that, Fabricius? Not one innocent man dead! [*On his way out, to* PARIS] There's not a moment to lose; we must show ourselves! [*Exit* DANTON *and* PARIS.]

ROBESPIERRE [*alone*]. Go then. He would rein in the steeds of the revolution at a brothel, as if he were a coachman and they a pair of docile hacks. Well, they'll have strength enough to drag him to the Place de la Révolution. Kick my stilts from under me, would he? Use my own terminology. Wait though. Is that the case? They'll say his enormous figure threw too broad a shadow on me, so I bundled him out of the sun. Will they be right? Is the whole thing so necessary? Yes, yes, the republic. He must go. It is ludicrous how my thoughts spy on each other. . . . He must go. When a crowd is pressing forward, a man standing still is as big a nuisance as if he were pushing in the opposite direction. He is trampled underfoot. We will not allow the ship of revolution to run aground on the shallow calculations and mudflats of these people. We must cut off the hand that presumes to hold it back; and should they hold on with their teeth, let the head go too. Away with a gang that has stripped the clothes from dead aristocrats and caught leprosy from them. No virtue? Virtue a pair of stilts? To use my own terminology. That keeps coming back. Why can't I be rid of the thought? He keeps pointing a bloody finger at the same place; no matter how much wadding I put round it the blood still seeps through. [*After a pause*] Some part of me, I don't know which, contradicts the rest. [*Goes to the window.*] Night snores over the earth and tosses in desolate dreams.

Thoughts, desires, hardly dreamt of, confused and formless, which shuddered away from the daylight, now take shape and crawl into the silent house of dreams. They open doors, look out of windows, they half become flesh. Limbs stretch in sleep, lips mutter. And isn't waking consciousness only a clearer dream? Are we not sleepwalkers? Are not our actions dream actions, only more sharply defined, more complete? Who will blame us for that? The mind performs more thinking acts in an hour than this sluggish organism, the body, can imitate in years. Sin is in the mind. Whether thought becomes action, whether the body carries it out, is mere chance.

[*Enter* SAINT-JUST.]

ROBESPIERRE. Hallo, who's there in the dark? Bring me light!

SAINT-JUST. Don't you know my voice?

ROBESPIERRE. Ah, it's you, Saint-Just!

[*A maid brings lights.*]

SAINT-JUST. Were you alone?

ROBESPIERRE. Danton has just left.

SAINT-JUST. I met him on the way. In the Palais Royal. He had his revolutionary face on and was speaking in epigrams. He was hob-nobbing with the *sans-culottes*, the whores were running at his heels and the mob stood whispering what he had said into each other's ears. We shall lose the advantage of attack! Are you going to hesitate any longer? We shall act without you. Our minds are made up.

ROBESPIERRE. What do you intend to do?

SAINT-JUST. We shall call a formal sitting of the three Committees: Legislative, Security, and Public Safety.

ROBESPIERRE. Very imposing.

SAINT-JUST. We must bury the great corpse with dignity. Like priests, not like murderers. We mustn't hack it up; all the limbs must go down together.

ROBESPIERRE. Speak more plainly.

SAINT-JUST. We must lay him out in full armour and slaughter his slaves and horses on his burial mound. Lacroix . . .

ROBESPIERRE. That perfect scoundrel; one-time barrister's clerk, now Lieutenant-General of France! Go on.

SAINT-JUST. Hérault-Séchelles.

ROBESPIERRE. A fine head.

SAINT-JUST. An engraved capital on the document of the Constitution. We don't need such fripperies any more. He'll be rubbed out. . . . Philippeau, Camille.

ROBESPIERRE. Camille too!

SAINT-JUST [*hands him a paper*]. Yes, I think so. Read that.

ROBESPIERRE. Oh, *Le Vieux Cordelier*![1] Is that all? He's only a boy; he's been making fun of you.

SAINT-JUST. Read this.   [*Points to a passage.*]

ROBESPIERRE [*reading*]. 'This bloody Messiah Robespierre between the two thieves Couthon and Collot[2] on a Calvary where he sacrifices and is not sacrificed. The prayerful sisters of the guillotine stand below like Mary and Magdalene. Saint-Just lies on his bosom like John the apostle and acquaints the Convention with the master's apocalyptic revelations. He holds his head like a monstrance.'

SAINT-JUST. I'll make him carry his like Saint Denis.

ROBESPIERRE [*reading on*]. 'Must we believe that this Messiah's sober frock coat is France's winding sheet? That his thin fingers twitching on the rostrum are the knives of the guillotine?—And you, Barère, who said that only coins would be struck off in the Place de la Révolution! But I shall not grope around in that old sack. He is a widow who's had half a dozen husbands and buried them all. Is it his fault if he has the gift of Hippocrates and can see death in a man's face six months before it comes? Who wants to sit down with corpses and smell their stink?' So, Camille, you too? Away with them. Quickly. Only the dead never come back. Have you the indictment ready?

SAINT-JUST. That's easily done. You laid down the broad lines to the Jacobins.

ROBESPIERRE. I was trying to frighten them.

---

[1] Moderate newspaper of which Camille Desmoulins was editor.
[2] Couthon and Collot d'Herbois were close associates of Robespierre.

SAINT-JUST. I need only carry out your threats. The forgers[1] will provide the *hors d'œuvre* and the foreigners[2] the dessert. They'll die of the meal, I promise you.

ROBESPIERRE. Quickly then, tomorrow! No long-drawn-out agony. I've grown squeamish these last days. Be quick.

[Exit SAINT-JUST.*]*

[*Alone*] Yes, a bloody Messiah who sacrifices and is not sacrificed. *He* redeemed men with His blood, and I redeem them with their own. He invented sin and I take it upon myself. He had the joys of suffering and I have the pangs of the executioner. Who denied himself more, He or I? But there's madness in that thought. Why must we keep looking over our shoulders at that one man? Truly the Son of Man is crucified in all of us; we all writhe in bloody sweat in the Garden of Gethsemane, but no man can redeem another with his wounds.—My Camille. They're all leaving me. Everything is empty and desolate. I am alone.

---

[1] Certain Jacobins, including Fabre d'Eglantine, Chabot, and Delaunay, who had been arrested for forging a document in order to enrich themselves.

[2] Arrested for financial speculation. Both they and the 'forgers' were in fact tried at the same time as Danton.

ACT TWO

Scene 1

A room.

DANTON, LACROIX, PHILIPPEAU, PARIS, CAMILLE DESMOULINS.

CAMILLE. Quickly, Danton. We haven't got time to kill.

DANTON [*dressing*]. But time will kill us. What a bore to put on a shirt every day. Then the breeches over it. To crawl into bed at night and out again in the morning. To keep setting one foot in front of the other, with no prospect of it ever changing. It's very sad. And to think that millions have done it before us and millions will do it again; and what's more, that we consist of two halves each doing identical things, so that everything happens twice over. It's very sad.

CAMILLE. You're talking like a child.

DANTON. Dying men often turn childish.

LACROIX. You're heading straight for perdition with your delays, and you'll take all your friends with you. Make it clear to the faint-hearts that it's time for them to rally round you. Call them in from the Mountain as well as the Plain.[1] Inveigh against the tyranny of the Decemvirs, talk daggers, invoke Brutus! That way you'll terrify the rank-and-file and rope in the lot, up to and including the Hébertiste suspects. You must give your anger free play. At least don't let us die disarmed and humiliated like the wretched Hébert.

DANTON. You've a bad memory. You called me a dead saint. You were more right than you thought. I went to the sections. They were very respectful—just like undertakers. I'm a relic, and relics are thrown in the gutter. You were right.

LACROIX. Why did you let things come to this?

DANTON. Let them? Yes, it's true. I got bored in the end. Always wearing the same coat, always pulling the same face—it's pitiful. To be so wretched an instrument, with one string always giving out the same note. I can't bear it. I wanted a comfortable billet. Well, I've got one.

---

[1] The Mountain ('La Montagne') was the Jacobins. The Plain ('La Plaine') was the deputies of the centre, committed neither to Jacobins nor Girondins.

The revolution is bringing me peace, but not the way I thought. Anyway, what support can I command? Our whores might take the matter up with the nuns of the guillotine. I can't think of anybody else. You can count them off on your fingers: the Jacobins have proclaimed virtue as the order of the day, the Cordeliers call me Hébert's executioner, the Commune is doing penance. The Convention—now that might be a way, but there'd be another 31st of May,[1] they wouldn't yield willingly. Robespierre is the dogma of the revolution; you can't put a pencil through him. It wouldn't work. We didn't make the revolution, the revolution made us. And even if it did work, I'd sooner lose my head than cut off other people's. I've had enough of it. Why should we human beings fight each other? We should sit down side by side and have peace. Something went wrong with us at the creation. Something is missing—I can't put a name to it but we won't find it in each other's guts. So why hack our bodies open looking for it? God, but we're wretched alchemists!

CAMILLE. Put in a more tragic vein that would run: How long must humanity devour its own members in everlasting hunger? Or: How long shall we shipwrecked mariners, adrift on this hulk, suck the blood from each other's veins in our unquenchable thirst? Or: Students of the algebra of flesh, seeking the unknown, eternally withheld X, how long must we write our equations in mutilated limbs?

DANTON. You're a strong echo.

CAMILLE. A pistol shot makes as much noise as a thunderclap, doesn't it? All the better for you; you should keep me by you.

PHILIPPEAU. And leave France to her executioners?

DANTON. What's the objection? It suits the people well enough. They are miserable: what more can a man ask to make him soft-hearted, noble, virtuous, or witty—or simply not bored? As if it mattered whether they die on the guillotine or from fever or old age! The guillotine's even to be preferred; they can step into the wings with limbs still supple, and strike pretty attitudes as they go off, and hear the spectators clap. It's very proper and just the thing for us; we can play-act all the way through, even though we're stabbed in good

---

[1] i.e., the Paris Commune would intervene. The battle between the Commune and the Convention over the Girondin members began on 31 May 1793.

earnest at the end. It's a good thing to shorten the life-span a bit. The coat was too long, our limbs were lost in it. Life becomes an epigram that fits. Who's got breath or wit enough for an epic in fifty or sixty cantos? It's time we started drinking our little dram of spirit out of liqueur glasses instead of butter barrels. At least now you get a mouthful; the other way you could hardly make the few drops run together in the hulking great tub. In any case I should have to cry out: It's too much of an effort for me! Life's not worth the trouble we take to hold on to it.

PARIS. Then make a break for it, Danton.

DANTON. Can you take your country with you on your boot soles? Oh, anyway—and this is the main thing—they'll never dare. [*To* CAMILLE] Come on, my boy, I tell you they won't dare. Adieu, adieu.

> [*Exeunt* DANTON *and* CAMILLE.]

PHILIPPEAU. There he goes.

LACROIX. And doesn't believe a word of what he said. Nothing but laziness. He'd sooner be guillotined than make a speech.

PARIS. What shall we do?

LACROIX. Go home and prepare to make a decent end, like Lucretia.

SCENE II
A promenade.

[*A* BALLAD SINGER, *a* BEGGAR,] *people walking.*
[*Enter* SIMON *and a* CITIZEN.]

CITIZEN. My good Jacqueline—I mean Corny . . . You know, Cor—

SIMON. Cornelia, citizen, Cornelia.

CITIZEN. My good Cornelia has blessed me with a little boy.

SIMON. Has borne a son to the republic.

CITIZEN. To the republic? That sounds a bit too general. People might think . . .

SIMON. But that's precisely it. The particular must give way to the general.

CITIZEN. My wife says that too.

BALLAD SINGER [*sings*]. Tell me then, tell me then,
　　　　　　　　What makes glad the hearts of men?

CITIZEN. I can't make up my mind about a name.

SIMON. Christen him Pike Marat.

BALLAD SINGER [*sings*]. Care and sorrow, care and sorrow,
　　　　　　　　Toiling from the earliest morrow
　　　　　　　　Till it's evening once again.

CITIZEN. I want three—there's something about the number three—and I'd like them to be useful and honest. I've got it—Plough Robespierre. But what about the third?

SIMON: Pike.

CITIZEN. Thanks, neighbour. Pike Plough Robespierre. Fine-sounding names.

SIMON. I tell you the breasts of your Cornelia, like the teats of the Roman she-wolf . . . No, that won't do. Romulus was a tyrant. It won't do.

[*They go off.*]

[*Enter two gentlemen.*]

BEGGAR [*singing*]. A clod of earth, a mossy plot . . .

Kind gentlemen, pretty ladies!

I GENTLEMAN. Find work, man. You look well enough fed.

2 GENTLEMAN. Here. [*Gives him money.*] The impudence! He has hands like velvet.

BEGGAR. Monsieur, how did you get your coat?

2 GENTLEMAN. Hard work. You can have as good a one yourself. See here, I'll give you work. Come to my house. I live . . .

BEGGAR. Monsieur: why did you do the work?

2 GENTLEMAN. To have the coat, you blockhead.

BEGGAR. You drudged for a bit of gratification. For a coat like that *is* gratification. A rag would do the job as well.

2 GENTLEMAN. Of course. It's the only way to get one.

BEGGAR. And I'm supposed to be the blockhead. It cancels itself out. It's sunny and warm on the street corner and life's easy.

[*Sings*]   A clod of earth, a mossy plot. . . .

[*Enter* ROSALIE *and* ADELAIDE, *followed by* SOLDIERS.]

ROSALIE [*to* ADELAIDE]. Quick, there are soldiers coming. We haven't had anything hot in us since yesterday.

BEGGAR.   Such will be my final lot.

Ladies, gentlemen!

SOLDIER. Halt, one, two! And where might you be off to, my dears? [*To* ROSALIE] How old are you?

ROSALIE. As old as my little finger.

SOLDIER. You're very sharp.

ROSALIE. And you're blunt.

SOLDIER. Then I'd better sharpen up on you, hadn't I?

[*Sings*]   Oh Christina, my Christina,
                 When we play the concertina,
                 Does it leave you feeling sore, sore, sore?

ROSALIE [*sings*]. Oh my soldier boy so sturdy,
                 When you grind your hurdy-gurdy
                 Then I only ask for more, more, more!

[*Enter* DANTON *and* CAMILLE.]

DANTON. Isn't it a picture? I can smell things in the air; the sun's been hatching out lechery. Wouldn't you like to jump into the middle of it all, tear your breeches off and tup them from behind like dogs in the street?

[*They pass by*.]

[*Enter a* LADY, *her daughter* EUGÉNIE, *a* YOUNG GENTLEMAN.]

YOUNG GENTLEMAN. Ah madame, the sound of a bell, the evening light on the trees, the twinkling of a star . . .

LADY. The scent of a flower! These natural pleasures, the pure enjoyment of nature! [*To her daughter*] You see, Eugénie, only virtue has eyes for these.

EUGÉNIE [*kissing her mother's hand*]. Maman! I have eyes only for you.

LADY. Good child.

YOUNG GENTLEMAN [*whispering in* EUGÉNIE'*s ear*]. Do you see that fine-looking woman with the old gent?

EUGÉNIE. I know her.

YOUNG GENTLEMAN. They say her hairdresser gave her a *coiffure à l'enfant.*

EUGÉNIE [*laughing*]. Wicked gossip!

YOUNG GENTLEMAN. The old gent has taken her out for a walk. He can see the bud swelling so he brings it out into the sunshine; he thinks he's the thunderstorm that made it grow.

EUGÉNIE. How improper! I've half a mind to blush.

YOUNG GENTLEMAN. That might make *me* turn pale.

[*Exeunt.*]

DANTON [*to* CAMILLE]. Don't expect anything serious from me, that's all! I just can't understand why people don't stop in the street and laugh in each other's faces. They ought to laugh out loud, at the windows above and the graves below. And the sky should burst and the earth spin with sheer laughter.

[*Exeunt.*]

1 GENTLEMAN. An astonishing discovery, I assure you. It changes the whole face of technology. Humanity is making giant strides towards its high destiny.

2 GENTLEMAN. Have you seen the new play? A tower of Babylon! A maze of arches, staircases, walkways, all put up as lightly and boldly as you please. One gets dizzy at every step. An odd feeling.

[*Stops, embarrassed.*]

1 GENTLEMAN. What's the trouble?

2 GENTLEMAN. Nothing. Your hand, monsieur. It's that puddle. Thank you. I could scarcely get past it. It could be dangerous.

1 GENTLEMAN. You weren't frightened?

2 GENTLEMAN. I was. The earth is a thin crust. I always think I might fall through where there's a hole like that. . . . You've got to step warily, it might break under you. But do go to the theatre, that's my advice.

SCENE III
A room.

DANTON, CAMILLE, LUCILE.

CAMILLE. I tell you, if they don't get things in wooden copies, all neatly labelled, in theatres, concerts, or art shows, they've got neither eyes nor ears for them. But carve a puppet, show them the hole where the string goes in, give it a pull so that its joints creak in blank verse with every step it takes—and then, what character-drawing, what verisimilitude! Take a little scrap of sentiment, an aphorism, a concept, dress it up in coat and trousers, give it hands and feet, paint its face and let it attitudinize through three acts till at the finish it gets married or blows its brains out—and lo, idealism! Fiddle out an opera that bears as much relation to the ups and downs of life as a clay pipe blowing bubbles to a nightingale—high Art. Turn people out of the theatre and on to the street—and oh dear me, how pitiful reality is! They forget God Almighty for his bad imitators. Creation, red-hot creation thunders and lightens in and around them at every moment; they hear and see nothing. They go to the theatre, they read poems and novels, they grimace like the puppets they find in them and turn up their noses at God's creatures. 'My dear, how commonplace!' The Greeks knew what they were talking about when they said that Pygmalion's statue came to life but bore no children.

DANTON. And artists treat nature as David treated the murdered Septembrists when they were thrown out of La Force on to the streets. He sketched them in cold blood and said: 'I'm catching the last spasm of life in these scoundrels.'

[*He is called away.*]

CAMILLE. What do you say, Lucile?

LUCILE. Nothing, I so love watching you when you speak.

CAMILLE. Do you listen as well?

LUCILE. Of course!

CAMILLE. Well, am I right? Do you really know what I said?

LUCILE. To tell you the truth, no.

[DANTON *returns.*]

CAMILLE. What's wrong?

DANTON. The Committee of Public Safety has decided to arrest me. I've just been warned and offered a place of refuge. They want my head. Well, they can have it. I'm fed up with these vexations. Let them take it. What does it matter? I shall know how to die with courage. It's easier than living.

CAMILLE. Danton, there's still time.

DANTON. Impossible, but I should never have thought . . .

CAMILLE. Your laziness!

DANTON. I'm not lazy, only tired. The soles of my feet are burning.

CAMILLE. Where are you going?

DANTON. Who can tell me that?

CAMILLE. But seriously, where?

DANTON. For a walk, my boy, for a walk.   [*Exit.*]

LUCILE. Camille.

CAMILLE. Hush, my dear.

LUCILE. When I think that they may take your head and . . . Camille, it's nonsense, isn't it? I'm crazy?

CAMILLE. Be calm. Danton and I aren't the same person.

LUCILE. The earth is broad and there are many things on it. Why just this one thing? Who would take it from me? It would be mean. And what could they want with it?

CAMILLE. I tell you again, you can be calm. I spoke to Robespierre yesterday. He was friendly. We're a little tense, it's true; different viewpoints, that's all.

LUCILE. Go and see him.

CAMILLE. We shared a bench at school. He was always moody and lonely. I was the only one to seek him out. Sometimes I even wrung a laugh from him. He's always shown me great affection. I'll go.

LUCILE. So quickly, *mon ami*? Go—but come here first. This [*kisses him*] and this. Now go. [*Exit* CAMILLE.]
It's a cruel time. Sometimes things happen like that. Who can find a way out? We just have to compose ourselves.

[*Sings*] Oh parting, parting, parting,
Who thought of parting first?

What made me think of that? It's bad that it should come into my head of its own accord. When he was going out I felt as though he'd never be able to turn round again, he'd just have to keep moving further and further away from me.—How empty this room is! The windows are open, as if a corpse had been laid out in it. I can't stand being here any longer.

[*Exit.*]

SCENE IV
Open country.

DANTON.

DANTON. I'm not going any further. I refuse to break this silence with the small talk of my footsteps and the wheezing of my breath. [*Sits down. After a pause*] I've heard tell of an illness that makes you lose your memory. Death is supposed to have something of that quality. Sometimes I have a wild hope that its effect is even stronger, that it deprives you of everything. If only that were so! Then I'd run like a Christian to save my enemy, that is my memory.—They say this place is safe—yes, for my memory. Not for me. The grave's a surer place for me—at least it brings oblivion. It would kill my memory. But here my memory lives and kills me. It or me—which? The answer is simple. [*Stands up, and turns round.*] I'm flirting with death. It's quite pleasant to make eyes at her from a distance, through a lorgnette. Really, the whole story's laughable. There's a sense of permanence in me that says, tomorrow will be the same as today, and the day after the same as that, and so on—nothing will ever change. It's all empty noise; they're trying to frighten me. They'll never dare! [*Exit.*]

SCENE V

A room. Night.

[DANTON, JULIE.]

DANTON [*at the window*]. Will it never stop? Will the light never be snuffed out, the noise never die? Will it never be silent and dark so that we don't have to watch and listen to each other's sordid little sins?—September!

JULIE [*calls from offstage*]. Danton! Danton!

DANTON. Yes?

JULIE [*coming in*]. What did you shout just now?

DANTON. Was I shouting?

JULIE. It was something about 'sordid little sins', then you groaned 'September'.

DANTON. I did? No, I said nothing. I hardly even entertained the thought —only the faintest shadow of a notion.

JULIE. You're trembling, Danton.

DANTON. Haven't I cause to tremble, with the walls so talkative? With my body so shaky that my thoughts stagger around using stone walls for lips? It's weird.

JULIE. Oh, George.

DANTON. Yes, Julie, it's very strange. I don't want to think any more if thoughts can turn to speech like that. Julie, there are some thoughts for which there should be no ears. It's bad that they should bawl like infants when they come into the world. It's bad.

JULIE. God preserve your reason, George. Do you recognize me?

DANTON. Why shouldn't I? You're a human being, a woman, my wife. And the earth has five continents, Europe, Asia, Africa, America, Australia, and twice two makes four. I'm quite sensible, you see? You said . . . *it* . . . shouted 'September'?

JULIE. Yes, Danton, I heard it all through the house.

DANTON. When I went to the window . . . [*Looks out.*] The city is quiet. All the lights are out. . . .

JULIE. There's a child crying near by.

DANTON. When I went to the window, there were voices shrieking in every street: 'September!'

JULIE. You were dreaming, Danton. Pull yourself together.

DANTON. Dreaming? Yes, I was dreaming, but there was something else. I'll tell you in a moment—my poor head's confused. A moment . . . Now I have it. I was riding the earth like a wild horse; it was careering breathlessly along and I, with gigantic limbs, clung to its mane and flanks. My head was thrown back and my hair streamed out into the void; thus it dragged me along. Then I screamed out in terror and woke up. I ran to the window—and then I heard it, Julie. —What does the word want? And among all possible words, why that one? What concern is it of mine? Why does it hold out its bloody hands to me? I never hurt it. Help me, Julie, my brain is numb. Wasn't it in September, Julie?

JULIE. The monarchs were only forty hours from Paris.

DANTON. The fortresses fallen, the aristos in the city.

JULIE. The republic was lost.

DANTON. Yes, lost. We couldn't have enemies behind our backs, we would have been fools. Two enemies on the same plank, us or them. The stronger pushes the weaker off—isn't that fair enough?

JULIE. Yes, yes.

DANTON. We struck them down. It wasn't murder, it was civil war.

JULIE. You saved the country.

DANTON. Yes, I did. It was self-defence, we had to do it. The man on the Cross took the easy way out: 'It must needs be that offences come, but woe to that man by whom the offence cometh!' *It must needs be*—this was that *must*! Who will curse the hand on which the curse of *must* has fallen? Who spoke that *must*? What is it in us that lies, whores, steals, and murders? We are puppets and unknown powers pull the strings. In ourselves, nothing, the swords with which spirits fight—only the hands are invisible, as in fairy tales . . . There, I'm quiet now.

JULIE. Perfectly quiet, my darling?

DANTON. Yes, Julie. Come to bed.

Scene VI

The street in front of DANTON's *house.*

SIMON, CITIZENS *in arms.*

SIMON. How late at night is it?

1 CITIZEN. What's that about the night?

SIMON. How late is it?

1 CITIZEN. Between sunset and sunrise.

SIMON. What time, you scoundrel!

1 CITIZEN. Look at your watch dial. Time for the old pendulum to go back and forth between the sheets.

SIMON. We must break in! Forward, citizens. Our heads will answer for it. Alive or dead. He's a violent man. I'll go first, citizens. Gangway for freedom! Look after my wife. I'll bequeath her a crown of oak leaves.

1 CITIZEN. A crown of acorns, more likely; that's the shape for her. They say she gets a few in her lap every day.

SIMON. Forward, citizens, you will put your country in your debt.

2 CITIZEN. I wish our country would do the same for us. Think of the holes we've made in other people's skins!—And it hasn't sewn up any in our breeches.

1 CITIZEN. Do you want it to sew up your flies?   [*Laughs.*]
                                                          [*The others laugh.*]

SIMON. Forward.

                    [*They force their way into* DANTON's *house.*]

Scene VII

The National Convention.

A group of DEPUTIES [LEGENDRE, ROBESPIERRE, SAINT-JUST].

LEGENDRE. Will this slaughter of deputies never stop? Who is safe if Danton falls?

1 DEPUTY. What can we do?

2 DEPUTY. He must put his case at the bar of the Convention. That's sure to succeed—what could they do against the power of his voice?

3 DEPUTY. Impossible. There's a decree preventing it.

LEGENDRE. It must be repealed, or an exception must be made. I'll propose the motion. I count on your support.

PRESIDENT. The session is open.

LEGENDRE [*mounts the rostrum*]. Four members of the National Convention were arrested last night. I am aware that Danton is one of them; the names of the others I do not know. But whoever they are, I demand that they be heard before the bar. Citizens, I declare that I consider Danton as blameless as myself, and I don't believe any reproach can be levelled at me. I have no wish to attack any member of the Committee of General Security or of the Committee of Public Safety; but I have good reason to fear that private animosity and private passion is depriving Liberty of a servant who has done the highest deeds on her behalf. The man whose energy saved France in 1792 deserves to be heard. If he is accused of high treason, he must be granted the right to reply.

[*Violent reactions.*]

SOME VOICES. We support Legendre's proposal.

1 DEPUTY. We are here in the name of the people. We cannot be torn from these benches without the consent of our electors.

2 DEPUTY. Your words smell of carrion; you took them from the mouths of the Girondins. Is it privilege you want? The axe of the law is poised over the heads of all.

3 DEPUTY. We cannot allow our own committees to withhold the asylum of the law from those who make the law, and send them to the guillotine.

4 DEPUTY. There is no asylum for crime, except when it wears a crown and sits on a throne.

5 DEPUTY. Only scoundrels clamour for the right of asylum.

6 DEPUTY. Only murderers refuse to recognize it.

ROBESPIERRE. This assembly has not known such confusion for many a
day. That proves that matters of moment are under discussion. Today will decide whether a few men are to carry off a victory over
their country. How can you so far deny your principles as to grant a
few individuals today what you refused yesterday to Chabot,
Delaunay, and Fabre? Why this discrimination in favour of a handful? Why should I concern myself with the praise men lavish on
themselves and their friends? Experience has taught us only too often
what such praise is worth. We do not ask whether a man has done
this or that patriotic deed; we ask after his whole political career.
Legendre appears not to know the names of the arrested men. The
whole Convention knows them. His friend Lacroix is one. Why does
Legendre seem not to know this? Because he is well aware that it is
mere impertinence to defend Lacroix. He named only Danton because he believes that is a privileged name. No! We will not have
privilege. We will not have idols! [*Applause.*] What advantage has
Danton over Lafayette or Dumouriez or Brissot? Over Fabre, Chabot,
Hébert? What can be urged against them that cannot also be urged
against him? Did you spare them? By what right does he deserve
preferential treatment from his fellow-citizens? Perhaps by right of
those few individuals, some dupes and some perfectly clear-headed,
who have followed him in his rush towards power and success. The
more he has deluded patriots who put trust in him, the more
sharply must he taste the severity of the friends of liberty.—They
want to make you afraid of misusing a power you have already
exerted. They howl at the despotism of the committees, as if the
trust which the people placed in you, and which you have vested in
those committees, were not a sure guarantee of their patriotism.
They act as if everyone went in fear and trembling. But I tell you
that whoever trembles at this moment is a guilty man; innocence
does not tremble before public vigilance. [*General applause.*] They
have tried to frighten me too. They gave me to understand that any
danger approaching Danton could also reach me. They wrote letters
to me, saying I was surrounded by friends of Danton, imagining that
the memory of an old association, the blind belief in a pretence of
virtue, could blunt my passionate zeal for liberty. I declare to you
now: nothing will stop me, not even if Danton's danger becomes my
own. We all need a little courage and magnanimity. Only criminals
and vulgar spirits fear to see their fellows fall by their sides, because
they then face exposure to the light of truth, with no mob of

accomplices to hide them. There may well be such spirits in this assembly; but there are also heroic ones. The number of scoundrels is not large. We need only strike off a few heads and the country is saved. [*Applause.*] I demand that Legendre's motion be rejected.

[*The delegates rise in a body to show their approval.*]

SAINT-JUST. There seem to be in this assembly some delicate ears which cannot stand the sound of the word 'blood'. A few general observations should convince them that we are not more cruel than nature or the times. Nature obeys her laws calmly and inexorably. Man is destroyed wherever he comes in conflict with her. A variation in the chemical composition of the air, an outbreak of subterranean fire, a change of balance in a body of water, and an epidemic, a volcanic eruption, a flood swallow up thousands. What is the result? A minor, scarcely perceptible alteration of physical nature which would have passed without a trace had it not left corpses in its wake. I ask you, shall mind in *her* revolutions be more squeamish than matter? May not an idea crush opposition as a law of physics does? Above all, shall a phenomenon which is completely remoulding moral nature, that is man, draw back at the sight of blood? History works through these arms of ours in the spiritual sphere just as, in the physical, it works through volcanoes and floods. What difference does it make if those men move their last in an epidemic or in a revolution? Humanity's steps are slow; they can be counted only by centuries. Behind each one rise the graves of generations. The advance to the simplest of discoveries, the most rudimentary of principles, has cost the lives of millions. Is it not obvious that at a time when the pace of history is faster, more men should get out of breath?—We come to a quick and simple conclusion. Since all men were created in the same circumstances, all men are equal—apart, of course, from those distinctions which nature herself has made; thus everyone is entitled to advantages but none to privileges, either as an individual or as a member of a group. Put this sentence of mine in real terms and you find that every clause has killed its men. The 14th July, the 10th August, the 31st May are its punctuation marks. It needed four years to be translated into physical terms, but in normal times it would have taken a century, and would have been punctuated with generations. Is it so remarkable that the stream of the revolution should at every bend and cataract cast up its corpses? We shall have further clauses to add to our sentence—are a few

hundred dead bodies to hold us back? Moses led his people through
the Red Sea and into the wilderness till the old corrupt generation
was exterminated, before he founded his new state. Legislators! We
have no Red Sea and no wilderness, but we have war and the guillotine. The revolution is like the daughters of Pelias; she dismembers
mankind to make it young. Humanity will emerge from the cauldron
of blood like the earth from the flood waters, with limbs primordially
strong, as though from a second creation!

[*Sustained applause. Some* DEPUTIES *stand up in their enthusiasm.*]
We call upon all the secret enemies of tyranny, throughout Europe
and the whole world, who carry the dagger of Brutus under their
cloaks, to share with us this sublime moment!

[*The spectators and* DEPUTIES *strike up the* Marseillaise.]

ACT THREE

Scene 1

The Luxembourg prison. A room with prisoners.

CHAUMETTE, PAINE[1], MERCIER, HÉRAULT-SÉCHELLES, *and other prisoners.*

CHAUMETTE [*plucking at* PAINE's *sleeve*]. You're probably right, Paine; at least I used to think so. But I've got a headache today, I feel quite odd. Help me with your arguments.

PAINE. Come then, philosopher Anaxagoras, I'll catechize you. There is no God; because either God made the world or He did not. If He did not, then the world contains its own origin and there is no God, because God is only God in that He embraces the origin of all being. However, God can *not* have created the world, because either the creation is eternal like God, or it has a beginning. If the latter is true, God must have created it at a specific point in time; in other words, having been quiescent for an eternity, He must have become active, that is He must have suffered a change in himself and become subject to the concept of time. But both concepts—change and time—are in conflict with the nature of God. Therefore God cannot have created the world. Now since we know that the world, or at least our own consciousness, exists, and since we know from what I've just said that our consciousness must have its origin either in itself or in something else that is not God, there can be no God. Q.E.D.

CHAUMETTE. You've given me light again. Thank you.

MERCIER. Just a moment, Paine. What if creation is eternal?

PAINE. Then it is no longer creation. It is one with God or an attribute of him, as Spinoza says. Because God is in all things, in you, my worthy friend, in the philosopher Anaxagoras, and in me. That wouldn't be so bad, but you must admit that it's not saying much for His Heavenly Majesty if he has to suffer toothache in each of us, or the clap, or to be buried alive, or at least have a highly disagreeable impression of these things.

MERCIER. But there must be a first cause.

[1] The author of *The Rights of Man* had been elected to the National Convention in 1792 by the department of Calais. He subsequently escaped the guillotine and was freed after Robespierre's fall in 1795. The views Büchner attributes to him are not typical.

PAINE. Who's denying it? But who would claim that this first cause is what we call God—that is, perfection? Do you maintain that the world is perfect?

MERCIER. No.

PAINE. Then how can you deduce a perfect cause from an imperfect effect? Voltaire did, but only because he didn't dare break with gods any more than with kings. A man who has nothing to fall back on but reason, and who lacks the knowledge or the nerve to use it logically, is a duffer.

MERCIER. I've a question to put against that. Can a perfect cause have a perfect effect? I mean, can perfection create perfection? Isn't that impossible, because the created thing can never contain its origin in itself, which according to you is the attribute of perfection?

CHAUMETTE. Stop, stop!

PAINE. Be calm, philosopher. You're quite right. But if God, once He starts creating, can create only imperfect things, then He'd better not bother. Isn't it very human of us that we can imagine God solely as a creator? Granted we have to keep shaking ourselves to prove that we really exist; but is that a reason for ascribing such a miserable need to God? Must we, every time we sink our spirit in the essence of a being eternally at peace, eternally blissful, assume straight away that its fingers itch to knead little dough-men, out of an invincible hunger for love, as we darkly whisper to each other? Why go through that rigmarole just to make ourselves out the sons of God? I prefer a lesser father; at least I can't reproach him with educating me beneath my station, in a pigsty or in the galleys. Do away with imperfection; that's the only way you'll prove the existence of God. Spinoza tried it. We can deny evil but not pain. Only reason can prove God. The senses reject Him. Take note, Anaxagoras. Why do I suffer? That is the rock of atheism. The least twinge of pain, should it convulse a single atom, splits creation from top to bottom.

MERCIER. And morality?

PAINE. First you prove God from morality and then morality from God! What's the point of your morality? I don't know whether there's anything good or bad *per se*. I don't have to change my way of life on that account. I act according to my nature. What suits it is good for me, and I do it. What's contrary to it is bad for me, and I don't do it and protect myself against it wherever I meet it. You can be virtuous, as they call it, and protect yourself against so-called vice, without having to despise your opponent, which is a pitiful state of mind.

CHAUMETTE. True, very true.

HÉRAULT. O philosopher Anaxagoras, one could also maintain that for God to be all He must also be His opponent, that is He must be perfect and imperfect, good and evil, blissful and suffering. Mind you, the result would be nil. He would cancel himself out, and we would end up with a zero. Rejoice, you've passed the examination. You can with a clear conscience worship Madame Mormoro as nature's masterpiece. She's obligingly left you a crown of thorns in your privates.

CHAUMETTE. Gentlemen, my grateful thanks.　　　　　　*[Exit.]*

PAINE. He still doesn't trust me. In the last analysis he'll take extreme unction, turn his feet towards Mecca, and have himself circumcised, just to take no chances.

　　　[DANTON, LACROIX, CAMILLE, PHILIPPEAU are brought in.]

HÉRAULT *[runs to DANTON and embraces him]*. Good morning . . . I should say, good night. I can't ask how you slept; but how *will* you sleep?

DANTON. At any rate, one must go to bed laughing.

MERCIER *[to PAINE]*. This mastiff with dove's wings! He's the evil genius of the revolution. He tried to violate his mother but she was stronger than he.

PAINE. His life and his death are equal calamities.

LACROIX *[to DANTON]*. I didn't think they'd come so soon.

DANTON. I knew; I was warned.

LACROIX. And you didn't say anything?

DANTON. What's the point? A stroke is the best death. Would you rather sicken first? Besides, I didn't think they'd dare. *[To* HÉRAULT.*]* It's better to lie down under the ground than give yourself corns walking on top of it. It makes a better pillow than a footstool.

HÉRAULT. At least we won't stroke the cheeks of the lovely lady putrefaction with horny hands.

CAMILLE [*to* DANTON]. Just don't make a fuss. You can stick your tongue out as far as your Adam's apple, it still won't lick the death-sweat from your forehead. O Lucile! This is a great affliction.

[*The prisoners crowd round the new arrivals.*]

DANTON [*to* PAINE]. What you did for the good of your country I tried to do for mine. I hadn't your luck; they're sending me to the scaffold. Let them. I won't stumble.

MERCIER [*to* DANTON]. You're drowning in the blood of the Girondins.

1 PRISONER [*to* HÉRAULT]. The power of the people and the power of reason are synonymous.

2 PRISONER [*to* CAMILLE]. Hey, procurator-general of the street-lamp! Your lighting improvements haven't made France any brighter.

3 PRISONER. Leave him alone. His are the lips which spoke the word 'Mercy'. [*Embraces* CAMILLE. *Several prisoners follow his example.*]

PHILIPPEAU. We are priests who prayed over the dying. We've caught their infection and are dying of the same complaint.

VOICES. The blow that falls on you will kill us all.

CAMILLE. Gentlemen, I deeply regret that our efforts were so fruitless. I go to the scaffold because my eyes watered at the fate of a few unfortunates.

SCENE II
A room.

FOUQUIER-TINVILLE, HERMAN.

FOUQUIER. Is everything ready?

HERMAN. It won't stand up. It would be simple if Danton weren't among them.

FOUQUIER. He must be first on the floor.

HERMAN. He'll terrify the jury, he's the scarecrow of the revolution.

FOUQUIER. The jury must be strong-willed.

HERMAN. I know a way, but it's against the letter of the law.

FOUQUIER. Tell us.

HERMAN. Don't draw lots. Pack the jury with sound men.

FOUQUIER. That ought to work—it's going to be quite a *feu de joie*: nineteen of them, and cunningly mixed. Four forgers, as well as a few bankers and foreigners. A tasty dish. Just what the people need.— Now then, reliable men. Who, for instance?

HERMAN. Leroi. He's deaf. He won't hear a word of what the accused say. Danton can scream himself hoarse as far as he's concerned.

FOUQUIER. Good. Next.

HERMAN. Vilatte and Lumière. One sits in the wineshop all day and the other is always asleep. Neither will open his mouth except to say 'Guilty'. Girard works on the principle that nobody who is brought before the tribunal should be allowed to go free. Renaudin . . .

FOUQUIER. He too? He once helped to get some priests off.

HERMAN. Don't worry. He came to me the other day and demanded that all condemned men should be bled before execution, to make them pale. They mostly look defiant and that annoys him.

FOUQUIER. Very good. I rely on you then.

SCENE III

The Conciergerie. A corridor.

LACROIX, DANTON, MERCIER, *and other prisoners walking up and down.*

LACROIX [*to another prisoner*]. What, so many unfortunates, and in such wretched conditions?

PRISONER. Have the tumbrils never told you that Paris is a slaughter-house?

MERCIER. Equality swings its sickle over the heads of all, the lava of revolution flows, the guillotine makes republicans, eh, Lacroix? The gallery claps, the Romans rub their hands; they don't hear that every word is the death-rattle of a victim. Follow your fine phrases through to the point where they become incarnate. Look around you: this is what you've been saying. It's all a mimic translation of your words. These wretches, their hangmen, and their guillotine are your speeches turned to life. You built your system, like the sultan Bajazet his pyramids, out of human heads.

DANTON. You're right. We do all our work these days in human flesh. It's the curse of our times. My body will be the next to go.—It's exactly a year since I set up the Revolutionary Tribunal. I cry pardon of God and man. My aim was to anticipate a new September massacre. I hoped to save the innocent. But this slow murder with its formalities is more horrible and just as inevitable. Gentlemen, I hoped to get you all out of this place.

MERCIER. We'll get out of it all right.

DANTON. Now I'm inside with you. Heaven knows how it will end.

SCENE IV
The Revolutionary Tribunal.

[DANTON *before* HERMAN *and the jury.*]

HERMAN [*to* DANTON]. Your name, citizen.

DANTON. The revolution names me. My place of residence will presently be oblivion and my name in the Pantheon of history.

HERMAN. Danton, the Convention accuses you of conspiring with Mirabeau, Dumouriez, Orléans, the Girondins, the foreigners, and the faction of Louis XVII.[1]

DANTON. My voice, which I have so often raised in the cause of the people, will easily refute this calumny. Let the wretches who accuse me appear in this court and I will heap them with shame. Let the Committees present themselves. I shall answer only to them. I need

[1] The Dauphin, then in prison, where he died in 1795. After Mirabeau's death in 1791 he was discovered to have been financed by the royal court abroad. Dumouriez, the victor of Valmy, was a constitutional monarchist and later defected to Vienna. The Duke of Orléans ('Philippe L'Égalité'), the brother of Louis XVI, was a liberal, but was guillotined in 1793 on suspicion of desiring to become constitutional King of France.

them both as prosecutors and as witnesses. Let them show themselves. —But what do I care for you and your judgement? I have told you already: oblivion will soon be my refuge. Life is a burden to me. Let them tear it from me, for I long to shake it off.

HERMAN. Danton, boldness is the mark of crime, serenity that of innocence.

DANTON. Private boldness is doubtless blameworthy; but that national boldness I have so often shown in the struggle for freedom is the most meritorious of virtues. That is *my* boldness; that is the quality which, for the good of the republic, I now turn against my pitiful accusers. Can I be calm when I see myself so vilely calumniated? Expect no cold defence from a revolutionary like me. Men of my stamp are beyond price in revolutions: the genius of liberty hovers on their brows.

[*Signs of applause among the audience.*]

I am accused of conspiracy with Mirabeau, Dumouriez, Orléans, of having grovelled at the feet of miserable despots. I am called upon to answer at the bar of inexorable, unbending justice. You, wretched Saint-Just, will be answerable to posterity for this calumny!

HERMAN. I call on you to answer calmly. Be mindful of Marat. He stepped before his judges with awe.

DANTON. You have laid hands on my whole life. Let it then rise up and oppose you. You will be crushed under the weight of my deeds. Not that I am proud of them; fate guides our arm. But only powerful natures are its instrument.—I declared war on kingship at the field of Mars. I defeated it on the 10th August.[1] On 21st January[2] I killed it and threw down a king's head as a gauntlet to other kings. [*Repeated applause. He holds up the bill of indictment.*] When I cast my eyes on this disgraceful document my whole being quivers. Who are these people who forced Danton to show himself on that memorable 10th August? Who are the privileged beings from whom he borrowed his energy? Let my accusers appear! I make this demand with a perfectly cool head. I will unmask the insipid rascals and hurl them back into the nothingness from which they should never have crawled.

[1] The storming of the Tuileries in 1792.
[2] The execution of Louis XVI.

HERMAN [*rings the bell*]. Don't you hear the bell?

DANTON. The voice of a man who defends his honour and his life cries louder than your bell. In September I fed the young brood of the revolution with the dismembered bodies of the nobility. My voice forged weapons for the people from the gold of the aristos and the rich. My voice was the hurricane that drowned the lackeys of despotism in a tidal wave of bayonets.   [*Loud applause.*]

HERMAN. Danton, your voice is exhausted. You are over-excited. You shall finish your defence another time. You need rest. The session is adjourned.

DANTON. Now you know Danton! A few hours more and he will fall asleep in the arms of fame.

SCENE V
The Luxembourg. A cell.

DILLON, LAFLOTTE, *a* GAOLER.

DILLON. Here, don't shine your nose in my face like that!   [*Laughs.*]

LAFLOTTE. And keep your mouth shut. Your moonface is bad enough without a halo of beery breath.   [*Laughs.*]

GAOLER [*laughs*]. Do you think, monsieur, that it's bright enough to read by?   [*Waves a piece of paper.*]

DILLON. Give it here!

GAOLER. The moon's on the wane, sir. My purse is at low water.

LAFLOTTE. Not by the look of your trousers. It's high tide down there.

GAOLER. They let the water in, not out. [*To* DILLON] Your sun has taken her light away, sir. You'll have to give her something to put colour in her cheeks if you want to read by her.

DILLON. Here, man. Now clear out. [*Gives him money. Exit* GAOLER.] [*Reads*] 'Danton has given the Tribunal a fright. The jury vacillated, the audience muttered. The crush was extraordinary. The people crowded round the Palais de Justice, as far back as the bridges.'

Oh, for a handful of money and a free arm! [*He walks up and down, pouring himself drinks from a bottle.*] One foot on the street, that's all I ask. I won't let myself be slaughtered like this. One foot on the street, that's all.

LAFLOTTE. Or in the tumbril; it amounts to the same thing.

DILLON. Think so? There are still a few steps between—enough to measure out with the bodies of the Decemvirs. The time has come at last for decent people to raise their heads.

LAFLOTTE [*aside*]. So they can be cut off the more easily. Keep it up, old chap; a few more glasses and you'll set me afloat.

DILLON. The scoundrels, the fools, they'll end up guillotining themselves. [*He paces up and down.*]

LAFLOTTE [*aside*]. A man could really love his life again, if, like his own child, he begot it himself. That doesn't often happen, to commit incest with chance and become your own father. Father and child at the same time. A comfortable sort of Oedipus!

DILLON. You can't feed the people with corpses. Danton's and Camille's wives should throw banknotes to the mob. That's better than heads.

LAFLOTTE [*aside*]. Only I wouldn't put my eyes out, like Oedipus. I might need them to weep for the poor old general.

DILLON. Laying hands on Danton. Who's safe after that? Fear will unite them.

LAFLOTTE [*aside*]. He's a doomed man. Where's the harm in treading on a corpse to climb out of the grave?

DILLON. One foot on the street and I'll find support enough. Old soldiers, Girondins, ci-devant nobles. We'll break open the prisons. We must come to terms with the prisoners.

LAFLOTTE [*aside*]. No doubt there's a slight smell of villainy about it. But what of that? I'd rather like to try it. I've been too one-sided till now. I'll get twinges of conscience, but they'll make a change. It's not unpleasant to smell your own stench. I've got bored with the prospect of the guillotine—all this waiting! I've been through it twenty times in my mind. It's lost its spice by now, and become quite common.

DILLON. We must get a letter out to Danton's wife.

LAFLOTTE [*aside*]. Besides, I'm afraid. Not of death, but of pain. There's no guarantee it doesn't hurt. They say it's only for an instant. But pain is a fine chronometer. It can anatomize a split second. No, pain is the only sin and suffering the only vice. I'll stay virtuous.

DILLON. Listen, Laflotte, where did that gaoler fellow get to? I have money; it's bound to work. The iron must be forged. My plan is ready.

LAFLOTTE. At once. I know the turnkey, I'll speak to him. Count on me, General, we'll get out of this hole ... [*Aside, going out*] into another. I into the widest one, the world; he into the narrowest, the grave.

Scene VI
The Committe of Public Safety.

SAINT-JUST, BARÈRE, COLLOT D'HERBOIS, BILLAUD-VARENNES.

BARÈRE. What does Fouquier write?

SAINT-JUST. The second hearing is over. The prisoners are demanding the appearance of several members of the Convention and the Committee of Public Safety; they appealed to the people against the refusal to allow witnesses. Apparently the commotion is beyond description. Danton parodied Jupiter and shook his locks.

COLLOT. The executioner will catch hold of them the more easily.

BARÈRE. We mustn't appear in public. The fishwives and the rag-pickers mightn't find us so impressive.

BILLAUD. The people have an instinct for being downtrodden, even if it's only with a look. They love these insolent faces. An arrogant brow is more dangerous than a coat-of-arms. The fine aristocracy of misanthropy sits on it. Every man who hates to be looked down on should help to smash them.

BARÈRE. Danton's like Siegfried; the blood of the Septembrists has made him invulnerable. What has Robespierre got to say?

SAINT-JUST. Nothing, but he acts as if he had. The jurymen must say they've taken all the evidence they need and close the debate.

BARÈRE. Impossible.

SAINT-JUST. They must be done away with at all costs, even if we have to strangle them with our own hands. Dare! Danton won't have taught us that word in vain. The revolution won't stumble over their bodies. But if Danton stays alive he'll catch her by the skirt-tails—and there's something in the set of the man that makes me think he'd commit a rape on liberty.

[*He is called away.*]

[*The* GAOLER *enters.*]

GAOLER. There are prisoners dying in St. Pélagie; they demand a doctor.

BILLAUD. Unnecessary. It'll save trouble for the executioner.

GAOLER. There are pregnant women among them.

BILLAUD. All to the good. Their children won't need coffins.

BARÈRE. A case of consumption among the aristos is a session the less for the Tribunal. To provide medicine would be counter-revolutionary.

COLLOT [*takes a paper*]. A petition. A woman's name.

BARÈRE. One of those who'd like to have to choose between the guillotine's head-rest and the bed of a Jacobin. They die after losing their honour, like Lucrece. Only a little later than the Roman lady—in childbirth, or of cancer or old age. It must be quite pleasant to drive a Tarquin out of the virtuous republic of a virgin.

COLLOT. She's too old. Madame is asking for death! Expresses herself too well: prison lies on her like the lid of a coffin. She's only been there four weeks. The answer is easy. [*He writes and reads*] 'Citizenness, desire death a little longer.'

[*Exit* GAOLER.]

BARÈRE. Well said. But, Collot, it's a bad thing for the guillotine to make jokes. People will stop fearing it. We mustn't become so familiar.

[SAINT-JUST *returns.*]

SAINT-JUST. I've just had a denunciation. There's a conspiracy in the prison; a young man called Laflotte discovered everything. He was in the same cell as Dillon. Dillon got drunk and blabbed.

BARÈRE. Cutting his throat with a broken bottle. It's happened before.

SAINT-JUST. Danton's and Camille's wives are to throw money to the people, Dillon is to make a break for it, the prisoners are to be freed and the Convention blown up.

BARÈRE. Fairy-tales.

SAINT-JUST. Just the thing to put them to sleep. I have the proofs in my hand. Add to that the arrogance of the accused, popular discontent, the jury's dismay—I'll make a report.

BARÈRE. Yes, go, Saint-Just. Spin your periods. Every comma is a sabre stroke, every full-stop a severed head.

SAINT-JUST. The Convention must establish the Tribunal's right to function without interruption. Any accused showing contempt for the dignity of the court or creating a disturbance will be excluded from the proceedings.

BARÈRE. You have an instinct for revolution. That sounds quite moderate but it will be effective. They can't keep silent. Danton will have to roar.

SAINT-JUST. I count on your support. There are people in the Convention as sick as Danton and who fear the same cure. They've got their spirit back, they'll scream about the violation of procedure. . . .

BARÈRE [*interrupting him*]. I'll say to them: in Rome the consul who discovered Catiline's conspiracy and put the criminals to death on the spot was accused of violating procedure. Who were his accusers?

COLLOT [*emotionally*]. Go, Saint-Just! The lava of revolution is on the move. Liberty will stifle in her embrace those weaklings who would have fertilized her mighty womb. The majesty of the people will appear to them in thunder and lightning, like Jupiter to Semele, and turn them to ashes. Go, Saint-Just, we will help you to hurl the thunderbolt on the cowards' heads.

[*Exit* SAINT-JUST.]

BARÈRE. Did you hear the word 'cure'? They'll end up prescribing the guillotine against the pox. It's not the moderates they're fighting, but vice.

BILLAUD. Till now the two have gone together.

BARÈRE. Robespierre is trying to make the revolution a conventicle and the guillotine a pulpit.

BILLAUD. Or a prayer-stool.

COLLOT. On which he'll soon be putting his head, not his knees.

BARÈRE. That will happen easily enough. The world really would be topsy-turvy if the so-called rascals were to be hanged by the so-called honest men!

COLLOT [*to* BARÈRE]. When are you coming to Clichy[1] again?

BARÈRE. When the doctor stops coming to me.

COLLOT. You must think a fiery comet stands over the place; its rays fairly burn up the marrow of your spine.

BILLAUD. Before long the charming Demaly's dainty fingers will be yanking it out of its scabbard and hanging it down his back like a pigtail.

BARÈRE [*shrugs his shoulders*]. Shh . . . Our virtuous friend mustn't get to hear about this.

BILLAUD. Bah, he's an impotent Masorete.

[*Exeunt* BILLAUD *and* COLLOT.]

BARÈRE [*alone*]. The monsters! 'Desire death a little longer.' The words should have withered the tongue that spoke them. And I . . .? When the hired ruffians broke into gaol to murder the Septembrists, one prisoner seized his knife and stabbed a priest in the heart. That saved his life! And where's the objection? What am I to do now—join the murderers or take my seat on the Committee of Public Safety? Reach for the guillotine or a pocket-knife? It's the same case, only a little more complex; the fundamentals are the same. And if our prisoner could kill one man, why not two, three, or even more? Where do you draw the line? It's the story of the barleycorns. How many make a heap—two? three? four? How many then? Come along, conscience, you prime pullet. Chucky-chucky-chucky-chuck! Here's fodder for you.—But was *I* a prisoner? I was under suspicion, and that's the same thing. I was certain of death. [*Exit.*]

---

[1] One of the country houses the republican leaders kept as private brothels.

SCENE VII
The Conciergerie.

LACROIX, DANTON, PHILIPPEAU, CAMILLE.

LACROIX. You roared beautifully, Danton. If you'd taken such pains about your life earlier things would be different today. But now death has come so brazenly close, it's so obtrusive; you smell its rotten breath, eh?

CAMILLE. If only it'd come like a rapist and tear its satisfaction from our hot limbs in a real fight. But these formalities! It's like marriage with an old woman. The banns are proclaimed, the witnesses called, Amen said, and then up with the counterpane and in she creeps with her frozen limbs.

DANTON. I wish it *were* a fight, with arms and teeth going. But I feel as if I'd fallen into a mill and my limbs were being twisted off, slowly, systematically, by cold physical power. To be killed so mechanically!

CAMILLE. And then to lie alone, cold, stiff, in the clammy vapour of putrefaction. Perhaps death flays the life slowly out of one's tissues. Pah! To rot to bits and be conscious of it!

PHILIPPEAU. Be calm, my friends. We are like autumn crocuses which bear seed only after the winter. We are transplanted flowers, the only difference being that we stink a little in the process. Is that so terrible?

DANTON. An edifying prospect. From one midden on to another! The divine classification according to Linnaeus, what? Prima to Secunda, Secunda to Tertia, and so forth. I'm fed up with the schoolbench, I've got welts on my arse like a monkey from sitting on it.

PHILIPPEAU. What do you want then?

DANTON. Rest.

PHILIPPEAU. That's in God.

DANTON. In *vacuo*. Plunge yourself in a greater peace than nothingness; and if the greatest peace of all is God, doesn't it follow that nothingness is God? But I'm an atheist. That damned argument: something cannot become nothing, there's the misery. Creation has become so broad, there's no emptiness. Everything is packed and swarming. The void has destroyed itself; creation is its wound. We are its drops of blood and the world the grave in which it rots. It sounds crazy, but there's truth in it somewhere.

CAMILLE. The world is the wandering Jew. Nothingness is death, but nothingness is impossible. Oh, never to lie down and die, as the song goes.

DANTON. We are all buried alive, laid out like kings in three- or four-fold coffins: first the sky, then our houses, then our coats and shirts. For fifty years we scratch at our coffin lids. If only a man could believe in annihilation, he'd be home and dry! But there's no hope in death; it's merely a simpler form of decomposition, life being a complex one. That's the entire difference. It just so happens that I'm used to this brand of putrefaction. The devil knows how I'll make out with the other.—Oh Julie, if I could go alone! If only she'd leave me to myself! Yet even if I were utterly dissolved and scattered, a handful of tormented dust, each atom of me could find its rest only in her. I cannot die. No, I cannot die! We must shout on to the end, they must wring the last drop of life from my limbs!

SCENE VIII
A room.

FOUQUIER, AMAR, VOULAND.

FOUQUIER. I've run out of answers. They're demanding a commission of inquiry.

AMAR. Here's what you were after. We've got the scoundrels.

[*Hands* FOUQUIER *a paper.*]

VOULAND. That will satisfy them.

FOUQUIER. We really needed that.

AMAR. To work, then; let's get this damned business off everybody's hands.

Scene ix
The Revolutionary Tribunal.

[DANTON *before the jury.*]

DANTON. The republic is in danger, and he has no instructions! We appeal to the people; my voice is still strong enough to pronounce the funeral oration of the Decemvirs. I repeat, we demand a commission. We have important disclosures to make. I will withdraw into the citadel of reason, I will debouch with the cannon of truth, I will shatter my enemies!   [*Signs of applause.*]

[FOUQUIER, AMAR, *and* VOULAND *enter.*]

FOUQUIER. Silence, in the name of the republic. In the name of the law! The Convention decrees: in view of the fact that signs of mutiny have appeared in the prisons, in view of the fact that the wives of Danton and Camille are distributing money to the people, and that General Dillon is plotting to escape and place himself at the head of an insurrection to free the accused; finally, in view of the fact that these latter have striven to provoke disturbances and bring the Tribunal into contempt, the Tribunal is empowered to continue its investigations without interruption and to exclude from its proceedings any of the accused who make light of the respect due to the law.

DANTON. I put it to those here present: have we flouted the Tribunal, the people, or the National Convention?

MANY VOICES. No! No!

CAMILLE. Wretches, they want to murder my Lucile!

DANTON. One day the truth will be acknowledged. I see a great misfortune overwhelming France. It is dictatorship. It has torn off its disguise, it carries its head high, it strides over our dead bodies. [*Pointing to* AMAR *and* VOULAND] There are the cowardly assassins, there are the ravens of the Committee of Public Safety! I accuse Robespierre, Saint-Just, and their hangmen of high treason. They wish to smother the republic in blood. The cart-ruts of the tumbrils are the highways by which foreign armies will thrust to the heart of our country. How long must the footprints of liberty be the graves of men? You want bread and they throw you heads! You thirst and they make you lap the blood from the steps of the guillotine!

[*Great excitement among the listeners. Shouts of applause.*]

MANY VOICES. Long live Danton! Down with the Decemvirs!

[*The prisoners are led away by force.*]

SCENE X

Square in front of the Palais de Justice.

A mob.

VOICES. Down with the Decemvirs, long live Danton!

1 CITIZEN. He was right! Heads for bread, blood instead of wine!

SOME WOMEN. The guillotine is a bad mill, and Samson the hangman a bad baker's boy. We want bread, bread!

2 CITIZEN. Danton has eaten your bread. His head will give all of you bread again. He was right.

1 CITIZEN. Danton was with us on the 10th August, Danton was with us in September. Where were his accusers then?

2 CITIZEN. Lafayette was with you in Versailles, but he was still a traitor.

1 CITIZEN. Who says Danton is a traitor?

2 CITIZEN. Robespierre.

1 CITIZEN. Then Robespierre is a traitor.

2 CITIZEN. Who says so?

1 CITIZEN. Danton.

2 CITIZEN. Danton has fine clothes. Danton has a lovely house. Danton has a beautiful wife. He takes his bath in burgundy, he eats venison off silver plates and sleeps with your wives and daughters when he's drunk. Danton was as poor as you are. Where did he get all this from? Veto the Sixteenth bought it for him, to save his crown! The Duke of Orléans gave it him to steal the crown. The foreigners bribed him with it to betray you all. What has Robespierre got, virtuous Robespierre? You all know him.

ALL. Long live Robespierre! Down with Danton! Down with the traitor!

ACT FOUR

Scene I
A room.

JULIE, a BOY.

JULIE. It's all over. He made them tremble. They are killing him from fear. Go to him and say I shall never see him again. I couldn't look at him . . . like that. [*Gives him a lock of her hair.*] There, give him this and tell him he won't go alone. He'll understand. And come back at once. I want to read his expression in your eyes.

[*Exit* BOY.]

Scene II
A street.

DUMAS, a CITIZEN.

CITIZEN. How can they condemn so many innocent men to death after such a hearing?

DUMAS. Indeed it's extraordinary. But the men of the revolution have an instinct that other men lack; it never lets them down.

CITIZEN. It's the instinct of the tiger. You have a wife.

DUMAS. I shall presently have had one.

CITIZEN. So it's true.

DUMAS. The Revolutionary Tribunal will pronounce our decree absolute. The guillotine will cut us off from bed and board.

CITIZEN. You are a monster.

DUMAS. Blockhead. Do you admire Brutus?

CITIZEN. With all my heart.

DUMAS. Does a man have to be a Roman consul with a toga to hide his head in, in order to sacrifice his nearest and dearest to his country? I shall wipe my eyes with the sleeve of my red coat; that's the only difference.

CITIZEN. That's horrible.

DUMAS. Be off. You don't begin to understand. [*Exeunt.*]

SCENE III
The Conciergerie.

LACROIX, HÉRAULT *on one bed*, DANTON, CAMILLE *on another.*

LACROIX. One's hair and nails grow so. It's enough to make one ashamed.

HÉRAULT. Watch what you're doing. You're sneezing grit all over my face.

LACROIX. And don't tread on my feet like that, my dear fellow. I've got corns.

HÉRAULT. You've got lice too.

LACROIX. I wish I could get rid of the worms.

HÉRAULT. Anyway, sleep well. We shall have to see how we get on together. There's not much room. And don't scratch me in your sleep. Ah . . . Don't pull at the grave-linen like that, it's cold down there.

DANTON. Yes, Camille, tomorrow we'll be a pair of broken shoes thrown in the lap of the beggar-woman Earth.

CAMILLE. The neat's leather from which, according to Plato, the angels have cut slippers to go shuffling about the world. It's just what one might have expected.—My poor Lucile.

DANTON. Take it easy, lad.

CAMILLE. Do you really think I'm able, Danton? Do you? They *can't* lay hands on her. The light of beauty that pours from her lovely body is inextinguishable. Look, the earth simply wouldn't dare to cover her; it would make an arch over her. The grave-damp would sparkle on her eyelashes like dew. Crystals would form like flowers round her limbs, and springs of clear water would murmur to her as she slept!

DANTON. Sleep, lad, sleep.

CAMILLE. Listen, Danton. Between ourselves, it's wretched to have to die. And it's useless! I want to snatch the last looks from the lovely eyes of life. I want to have my eyes open.

DANTON. They'll be open anyway. Samson doesn't bother to press the lids down. Sleep is more merciful. Sleep, my boy, sleep.

CAMILLE. Lucile, your kisses breed like imagination on my lips. Every kiss becomes a dream; then my eyes close and shut it safely in.

DANTON. Will the clock not be still? With every tick it slides the walls closer round me, till they're as narrow as a coffin. I once read a story like that as a child. It made my hair stand on end. Yes, as a child. What a waste of time fattening me up and keeping me warm! Mere work for the grave-diggers. I feel as if I were rotten already. My dear carcass, I'll hold my nose and make believe you're a girl all smelly and sweating after a dance and pay you compliments. We used to have better times together. Tomorrow you'll be a broken fiddle, with no tune left in you. Or an empty bottle—the wine's drunk but I'm not; I have to go sober to bed. Lucky people who can still get drunk! Tomorrow you'll be a worn-out pair of pants— you'll be thrown in the wardrobe and the moths will eat you whether you're stinking or not.—Ah, it's no good. Dying *is* a wretched business. It apes birth. Dying, we're as naked and helpless as new-born infants. We're given a shroud as a napkin. But it's no help. We can grizzle in the grave as well as in the cradle. Camille! He's asleep. [*Bending over him*] There's a dream playing between his eyelashes. I'll not brush the golden dew of sleep from his eyes. [*Stands up and walks to the window.*] I shan't go alone. Thank you for that, Julie. Yet I'd have liked to die differently, effortlessly, like a falling star, like a note fading away, kissing itself to death with its own lips, like a ray of light burying itself in clear water. The stars are sprayed across the night like shimmering tears; there must be great grief in the eye that shed them.

CAMILLE [*sits bolt upright, groping for the ceiling*]. Ahhh!

DANTON. What is it, Camille?

CAMILLE. Oh! Oh!

DANTON [*shaking him*]. Are you trying to claw the roof down?

CAMILLE. Oh, it's you! Hold me. Speak to me.

DANTON. You're trembling in every limb. There's sweat on your forehead.

CAMILLE. That's you, this is me. So far so good . . . Here's my hand.—Now I remember. Oh, Danton, it was horrible.

DANTON. What was?

CAMILLE. I was half awake, half dreaming. Then the ceiling vanished and the moon came down, closer and closer, till I could hold it in my arms. The sky with all its lights had sunk right down—I heaved against it, I fumbled with the stars, I reeled like a drowning man under a layer of ice. It was terrifying, Danton.

DANTON. The lamp throws a circle of light on the ceiling. That's what you saw.

CAMILLE. Damn what I saw. It doesn't take much to make us lose the few wits we have. Madness had me by the hair. [*He stands up.*] I won't sleep any more—I don't want to go crazy. [*Reaches for a book.*]

DANTON. What one are you taking?

CAMILLE. Young's *Night Thoughts*.

DANTON. Do you want to die in advance? I'll take *La Pucelle*[1]. I won't sneak out of life as though it was a prayer-stall, no! From the bed of a sister of mercy rather. Because life is a harlot; she fornicates with the whole wide world.

SCENE IV
Square before the Conciergerie.

A GAOLER, *two* CARTERS *with tumbrils, women.*

GAOLER. Who said you were to come here?

I CARTER. *Who!* That's a funny name to give a man.

GAOLER. You dolt, who commissioned you to come?

I CARTER. Commission? We don't get no commission. Only a measly ten sous a head.

2 CARTER. This bugger would take the bread out of our mouths.

[1] Mock-heroic poem by Voltaire on the subject of Joan of Arc, strongly anti-religious in tone.

1 CARTER [*pointing to the window of the prisoners' cell*]. What do you call bread? This lot's food for worms.

2 CARTER. How about my kids? They're little wrigglers too; they want their share. Business is lousy, even for the best, like us.

1 CARTER. How do you make out we're best?

2 CARTER. Well, who *is* the best carter?

1 CARTER. The one that takes you furthest and fastest.

2 CARTER. Well, bright boy, nobody can go further than out of this world and we do the trip in a quarter of an hour. It's exactly fifteen minutes from here to the Place de la Révolution.

GAOLER. Get a move on, you scoundrels. Come closer to the gate. Make way, girls!

1 CARTER. No, stay where you are. With women it's no good going round the side. Always up the middle!

2 CARTER. You bet. Cor, there's room for a horse and cart up this bunch. No trouble finding the rut there. But you'll have to go into quarantine when you come out.   [*They drive forward.*]

[*To the women*] What are you gaping at?

WOMAN. We're waiting for old customers.

2 CARTER. Do you think my cart's a whorehouse? It's a respectable cart, it drove the King and all the nobs of Paris to their last dinner out.

[*Enter* LUCILE. *She sits on a stone under the prisoners' window.*]

LUCILE. Camille! Camille!   [CAMILLE *appears at the window.*]
Listen, Camille, you make me laugh with your long stone coat-front and that iron mask in front of your face. Can't you bend down to me? Where are your arms? I'll tempt you down, dear little bird.

[*Sings*]   Two stars are shining in the sky
             Far brighter than the moon—
             One shines in at my sweetheart's window,
             The other at her chamber door.

Come, *mon ami*. Quietly up the stairs, they're all asleep. It's been a long wait but the moon's been helping me pass the time. But you can't get through the door in those awful clothes. Oh, the joke's too cruel, stop it! You just don't move. Why won't you say something? You frighten me. Listen, people are pulling long faces and saying you must die. I can't help laughing at their faces. Die. What sort of word is that, tell me, Camille? Die. I must think it over. Look, there it is. I'm going to run after it. Come, my darling, help me catch it!

[*She runs away.*]

CAMILLE [*shouting*]. Lucile! Lucile!

Scene v
The Conciergerie.

DANTON *at a window that looks into the next room.* CAMILLE, PHILIPPEAU, LACROIX, HÉRAULT.

DANTON. You're quiet now, Fabre.

VOICE [*from offstage*]. Deathly quiet.

DANTON. Do you know what we're doing now?

VOICE. What?

DANTON. What you've done all your life—*nous faisons des vers.*

CAMILLE [*aside*]. There was madness at the back of her eyes. More people have been going mad, it's the way of the world. What can we do but wash our hands of it? It's better so.

DANTON. I shall be leaving everything in a horrible mess. Nobody understands the least thing about government. It might still work out if I left Robespierre my whores and Couthon my legs.

LACROIX. They say we made liberty a harlot.

DANTON. That's of no consequence. Freedom and a whore are the two most cosmopolitan things under the sun. Now she'll ply her trade between the respectable sheets of the Arras lawyer. But I think she'll play Clytemnestra with him. I don't give him six months. I'll drag him with me.

CAMILLE [*aside*]. Heaven help her to a comfortable delusion. The general run of delusion, which we call sanity, is intolerably boring. The happiest man has always been the one who thinks he's God the Father, Son, and Holy Ghost.

LACROIX. The morons will shout 'Long live the republic' when we go past.

DANTON. What of that? Let the flood of the revolution cast up our bodies where it chooses. Our fossilized bones will still serve to crack the skulls of the kings.

HÉRAULT. Yes, so long as there's a Samson to swing our jaw-bones.

DANTON. They're all false brothers, like Cain.

LACROIX. Robespierre's a Nero, and nothing proves it more clearly than the fact that he was at his most affable with Camille two days before his imprisonment. Isn't that so, Camille?

CAMILLE. Maybe so, I don't care. [*Aside*] What an adorable child she has borne to madness. Why must I be shuffled off now? We might have laughed together with it, and dandled it and kissed it.

DANTON. When history comes to open its graves, despotism may yet choke on the smell of our corpses.

HÉRAULT. We stank enough when we were alive. You're making phrases for posterity, Danton. They're no concern of ours.

CAMILLE. He's making a face as if he expected to petrify and be dug up by posterity as an antique.—It's lost labour, all this rant and grease-paint and talking posh. We should all unmask; then it would be like a room full of mirrors, we'd see everywhere the same age-old indestructible sheep's head repeated to infinity. Nothing else. The differences are so small. We're villains and angels, geniuses and boneheads, all in one. There's room for all four in the same body; they're not on the scale people imagine. Sleep, digest, and make babies—we all do these things. What's left is only variations; the key changes, but the theme's the same. And for that we creep around on tiptoe making wry faces and feeling embarrassed. We've all eaten ourselves sick at the same table and now we've got bellyache—so why hide your face behind your napkin? Moan and groan as the fancy takes you. And don't contort your features into a caricature of virtue or wit or heroism or genius. We all know each other here. Save yourself the trouble.

HÉRAULT. Yes, Camille, let's sit down together and moan. How stupid to stay tight-lipped when you're being hurt. Greeks and gods cried out, Romans and Stoics put on heroic faces.

DANTON. The ones were as good Epicureans as the others. They all got their cosy glow of self-satisfaction. There's nothing wrong with wrapping your toga round you to see how long a shadow you throw. Why should we torment ourselves? Does it matter if we deck our genitals with bay leaves, rosary beads, or vine-leaf posies, or carry the ugly things openly for the dogs to lick?

PHILIPPEAU. Friends, we don't need to soar very high above the earth to lose sight of this chaos of fluctuation and uncertainty and have our eyes filled with a few great godly outlines. There is an ear for which the clamour and discord which deafen us are a stream of harmonies.

DANTON. But we're the poor musicians and our bodies the instruments. Do we wring these awful yowlings from them only to have them rise higher and higher and fade away into a voluptuous sigh in the ears of heaven?

HÉRAULT. Are we sucking pigs, caned to death to make our flesh the tastier for princely tables?

DANTON. Are we children, roasted in the hot Moloch-arms of the world and teased with rays of light so that the gods may enjoy their laughter?

CAMILLE. Is the ether with its golden eyes, the stars, a dish of golden carp on the table of the blessed gods? And do the gods everlastingly laugh and the fish everlastingly die? Do the gods take never-ending pleasure at the play of colours in their death agony?

DANTON. The world is chaos. Nothingness is the world-god yet to be born.

[*Enter* GAOLER.]

GAOLER. Gentlemen, you may take your leave. Your carriages await.

PHILIPPEAU. Friends, good night. Let us calmly pull over us the great coverlet under which all hearts cease to beat and all eyes fall shut.

[*They embrace.*]

HÉRAULT [*takes* CAMILLE'*s arm*]. Take comfort, Camille. We shall have a fine night. The clouds are hanging in a quiet evening sky like a cooling Olympus full of pale foundering gods.

[*Exeunt.*]

SCENE VI
A room.

JULIE.

JULIE. The people were running in the streets. Now everything is silent. I don't want to keep him waiting, not for a moment. [*Takes out her phial.*] Come, dear priest. Your Amen sends us to bed. [*Goes to the window.*] It's so pretty to say good-bye. Now I've only to shut the door behind me. [*She drinks.*]—I should like to stand like this forever. The sun has gone down. The earth's features were so sharp in its light, but now her face is as calm and grave as a dying woman's. How beautifully the evening light plays on her forehead and cheeks. She turns paler and paler, she drifts like a corpse down the river of space. Will no arm catch her by her golden hair and pull her from the water and bury her?—I'll walk softly. I won't kiss her, in case a breath or a sigh should waken her. Sleep . . . Sleep . . .

[*She dies.*]

SCENE VII
Place de la Révolution.

Tumbrils drive up and stop by the guillotine. Men and women singing and dancing La Carmagnole. *The prisoners strike up the* Marseillaise.

1 WOMAN [*with children*]. Gangway. Gangway. The children are complaining, they're hungry. I've got to let them see, to keep them quiet. Gangway.

2 WOMAN. Hey, Danton, now you can fornicate with the worms.

3 WOMAN. Hérault! I'll have a wig made from your pretty hair.

HÉRAULT. I haven't enough to reafforest a mount of Venus as bald as yours.

CAMILLE. Damned hags! You'll live to say to the mountains, Fall on us, and to the hills, Cover us.

2 WOMAN. The mountain's on you, mate!

DANTON. Calm, my lad. You've shouted yourself hoarse.

CAMILLE [*gives the* CARTER *money*]. Here, old Charon. Your cart is an excellent salver. Gentlemen, I shall serve myself first. It's a classical banquet. We lie down in our places and sprinkle a little blood as a libation. Adieu, Danton.
[*He ascends the scaffold. The prisoners follow him one by one,* DANTON *last.*]

LACROIX [*to the people*]. You're killing us on the day you've lost your reason. You'll kill *them* on the day you get it back.

VOICES. That's been said before. What a bore.

LACROIX. The tyrants will trip on our graves and break their necks.

HÉRAULT [*to* DANTON]. He thinks his corpse is a compost-bed for freedom.

PHILIPPEAU [*on the scaffold*]. I forgive you. I hope your hour of death may be no bitterer than mine.

HÉRAULT. I thought as much. He has to open his shirt-front again to show people he has clean linen.

FABRE. Good luck, Danton. I'm dying twice over.

DANTON. Adieu, my friend. The guillotine is the best physician.

HÉRAULT [*tries to embrace* DANTON]. Ah, Danton, I can't so much as crack a joke. The time has come.   [HANGMAN *pushes him back.*]

DANTON [*to the* HANGMAN]. Would you be more cruel than death? You can't prevent our heads from kissing in the basket.

SCENE VIII
A street.

LUCILE.

LUCILE. And yet there *is* something serious in it. I must think. I'm
beginning to grasp it. . . . To die. Die. Everything has the right to
live, everything—the little fly there, that bird. Why not he? The
river of life would stop if a single drop were spilled. That blow would
give the whole earth a wound.—Everything moves. Clocks tick, bells
peal, people walk, water trickles, everything—except in that one
place. No! It can't be allowed to happen. I shall sit on the ground and
scream until everything stops in fright and nothing moves any more.
[*Sits down, puts her hands over her eyes and screams. Pause. She gets up.*]
It's no good. Everything is just as before: the houses, the street, the
wind blowing, the clouds passing. We shall just have to bear it.

[*Some women come down the street.*]

1 WOMAN. A handsome man, that Hérault.

2 WOMAN. When he was standing at the triumphal arch at the festival
of the Constitution I said to myself: that one'll know how to conduct
himself on the guillotine, I said. What you might call a presentiment,
it was.

3 WOMAN. Yes, you've got to see people on their bad days as well as
their good. A very good thing that they've made dying public, I say.

[*They pass by.*]

LUCILE. My Camille! Where shall I look for you now?

SCENE IX
Place de la Révolution.

Two EXECUTIONERS *at work on the guillotine.*

1 EXECUTIONER [*standing on the guillotine, sings*].
            I came home one night,
            When the moon shone bright,
            And my grand-dad he did say . . .

2 EXECUTIONER. Hey, you. Ain't you done yet?

I EXECUTIONER. In a minute.

[*Sings*]   A-whoring, a-whoring,
                  Where have you been a-whoring . . . ?
  Here, give me my coat.
                  The whores will be your ru-i-in,
                  One fine day.

[*Exeunt singing.*]

[LUCILE *enters and sits on the steps of the guillotine.*]

LUCILE. You silent angel of death, let me sit in your lap.

[*Sings*]   Behold the reaper, death by name,
               His power from highest heaven came.

You cradle, who rocked my Camille asleep and stifled him among your roses. You passing bell whose sweet tongue sang him to his grave.

[*Sings*]   Souls beyond number, one and all,
                  Under his mighty sickle fall.

[*Enter a patrol.*]

CITIZEN. *Qui va là!*

LUCILE [*reflects a moment, then suddenly decides*]. Long live the King!

CITIZEN. In the name of the republic!

[*The watch surround her and take her away.*]

LEONCE AND LENA
A Comedy
[1836]

Prologue:

ALFIERI: *E la Fama?*

GOZZI: *E la Fame?*

DRAMATIS PERSONAE

KING PETER, of the kingdom of Po

PRINCE LEONCE, his son

VALERIO

LEONCE'S TUTOR

MASTER OF THE REVELS

LORD PRESIDENT OF THE COUNCIL

COURT CHAPLAIN

A MAGISTRATE

A SCHOOLMASTER

PRINCESS LENA, of the kingdom of Pee

LENA'S GOVERNESS

ROSETTA

Valets de chambre, servants, privy counsellors, ladies, gentlemen, peasants, etc.

ACT ONE

Oh that I were a fool!
I am ambitious for a motley coat.
As You Like It

SCENE I
A garden.

PRINCE LEONCE, *reclining on a bench*; TUTOR.

LEONCE. Well, sir, what is it you want with me—to prepare me for my calling? But I've got my hands full, I don't know which way to turn for work.—You see, first I have to spit on this stone three hundred and sixty-five times consecutively. Ever tried it? You ought to, it's a unique form of entertainment. Then—do you see this handful of sand?   [*He scoops up some sand, throws it in the air and catches it on the back of his hand.*]

First I throw it in the air. Now, shall we have a little wager—how many grains on the back of my hand? Odd or even? What, you won't bet? Are you a heathen? Do you believe in God? I usually wager against myself; I can keep it up all day. If you could conjure up somebody willing to bet with me occasionally you'd greatly oblige me. Then I have to devise a method of seeing the top of my head. Oh, to be able to see the top of one's head! It's an ideal of mine. It would be a great comfort. *Now* am I idle? *Now* have I no occupation?—Yes, it's sad . . .

TUTOR. Very sad, Your Highness.

LEONCE. . . . that the clouds have been blowing from west to east for the past three weeks. It makes me quite melancholy.

TUTOR. Very justifiably so.

LEONCE. Damn it, why don't you contradict me? Haven't you got a pressing appointment? I'm sorry I've detained you so long.

[*The TUTOR departs with a low bow.*]

Sir, I congratulate you on the fine pair of brackets your legs make when you bow.

[*Alone, he stretches himself out on the bench.*]

The bees sit so drowsily on the flowers, the sunshine lies so lazily on the earth. An appalling idleness rages. Sloth is the root of all vice. The things people do from boredom! They study from boredom, they pray from boredom; they fall in love, marry, and multiply from boredom, and finally they die of boredom. And the funny thing is that they do it with the gravest of faces, without knowing why. God knows what's in their heads. All your heroes, geniuses, dunderheads, your saints and sinners and fathers of families, are at bottom nothing but sophisticated idlers.—Why do *I* have to realize that? Why can't I take myself seriously and dress up the poor puppet in morning coat and umbrella and let it be nice and respectable and useful and high-minded? That fellow who's just left me—I envied him, I could have cudgelled him from sheer envy. If only one could become somebody else, just for a minute.

[*Enter* VALERIO, *rather drunk.*]

How the fellow runs! I wish I knew of a single thing under the sun that would make me run.

VALERIO [*plants himself in front of the Prince, lays his finger on his nose and stares at him*]. Absolutely.

LEONCE [*does the same*]. Quite right.

VALERIO. Have I made myself clear?

LEONCE. Perfectly.

VALERIO. In that case we'll change the subject.

[*He lies down on the grass.*]

In the meantime I shall lie on the ground and allow my nose to peep out between the grass blades. When the bees and butterflies rock themselves upon it, as upon a rose, I shall receive poetical impressions.

LEONCE. Then don't sniff so, my dear fellow. Otherwise you'll snuff the pollen out of the flowers and the bees and butterflies will starve.

VALERIO. How I feel for nature, sir. The grass stands up so prettily that one could wish to be an ox to eat it, and then a man again to eat the ox that had eaten such grass.

LEONCE. Unhappy man, you too are afflicted by ideals.

VALERIO. It's tragic. One can't jump off a church spire without breaking one's neck. One can't eat four pounds of cherries, including stones, without getting bellyache. Truly, sir, I could sit in a corner from night till morning singing: 'I can see a fly on the wall, fly on the wall, fly on the wall' etcetera for the rest of my life.

LEONCE. Shut up with your song. It's enough to drive one mad.

VALERIO. At least that would be something. A madman. Who will barter his madness for my good sense?—There, now I'm Alexander the Great. The sunshine crowns my hair with gold; my uniform glitters. Generalissimo Grasshopper, sound the advance! Lord Chancellor Spider, I require money! Dear Lady Dragonfly, what is my beloved spouse Queen Lamp-post doing? And, most excellent Doctor Spanish Fly, I'm in need of an heir. For this kind of charming fantasy a man can have good soup, good beef, good bread, a good mattress and a free haircut, I mean in the madhouse; whilst I with my sound wits can do no more than hire myself out as a ripener of cherry trees—and to what end?

LEONCE. To make the cherries blush at the view through the holes in your breeches. But, most noble sir, what is your trade, profession, occupation, state, or craft?

VALERIO [*dignified*]. Sir, my occupation is the weighty one of idleness. I am uncommonly versed in the art of doing nothing. I have colossal stamina in the pursuit of sloth. No welts disfigure my hands; the earth has drunk no sweat from my brow. Where work is concerned I am a virgin, and if it wasn't too much trouble I should take pains to expatiate to you at greater length upon these accomplishments.

LEONCE [*with mock enthusiasm*]. Come to my bosom! Art thou one of those godlike creatures who wander effortlessly, with untroubled brow, through the dust and sweat of the highway of life, who enter Olympus with shining foot-soles and bodies at their prime like the blessed gods? Come!

VALERIO [*sings as he makes his exit*]. I can see a fly on the wall, fly on the wall, fly on the wall. . .

[*Both off, arm in arm.*]

Scene II
A room.

KING PETER, *two* VALETS DE CHAMBRE.

KING PETER [*while being dressed*]. Man must think, and I must think for my subjects. Because they never think. Now the substance of a thing is the thing in itself, that is to say me.

> [*He walks around the room half naked.*]

Have you got that? The thing in itself is in itself, do you follow? Then we can go on to my modes, attributes, affects, and accidentals: where are my shirt and trousers? Shame on you, you've left my free will exposed down the front there. Where's morality? Where are my cuffs? The categories are in a scandalous state of confusion: you've buttoned two buttons too many and my snuffbox is in my right-hand pocket. My entire system is ruined. Ah, a knot in my handkerchief—what does that mean? You, fellow, what was I trying to remind myself of?

I VALET. When Your Majesty was pleased to tie this knot in your handkerchief, Your Majesty wished . . .

KING PETER. Well?

I VALET. To remind yourself of something.

KING PETER. A complex answer. Indeed. And what do you mean by that?

2 VALET. When Your Majesty was pleased to tie this knot in your handkerchief, Your Majesty wished to remind yourself of something.

KING PETER [*walking up and down*]. But what? These fellows are confusing me. I'm in the greatest perplexity, and I don't know what to do about it.

> [*Enter a* SERVANT.]

SERVANT. Your Majesty, the Privy Council is assembled.

KING PETER [*joyfully*]. That's it! I've got it. I wanted to remind myself of my people.—Come, gentlemen. Walk symmetrically. Isn't it very hot? Kindly take out your handkerchiefs and wipe your faces. I always get into a state when I have to speak in public.

> [*All off.*]

[KING PETER *and the* PRIVY COUNCIL *return.*]

KING PETER. My dear and loyal subjects. Know all men by these presents,
by these presents . . . because either my son will marry or he will
not . . . [*Puts his finger to his nose.*] Either/or, you understand me?
There is no third possibility. Man must think. [*Stands musing for a
while.*] When I speak out loud like that I don't know whether it's
really me or somebody else. That alarms me. [*After long reflection*]
I am I. What's your opinion, my Lord President?

LORD PRESIDENT [*slowly and with gravity*]. Your Majesty. It may be so,
and then again it may not.

PRIVY COUNCIL [*in a chorus*]. It may be so, and then again it may not.

KING PETER [*moved*]. Oh, my wise men! Now what were we talking
about? What was I going to say? My Lord President, how is it that
you have so short a memory on such a solemn occasion? The sitting
is adjourned.

[*He walks solemnly off, followed by the* COUNCIL.]

SCENE III

A richly decorated hall. Candles burning.

LEONCE *and* SERVANTS.

LEONCE. Are all the shutters closed? Light the candles, away with day!
I want night, deep ambrosial night. Put the lamps under crystal bells
and scatter them among the oleanders; let them dream there like
girls' eyes under the lashes of the leaves. Bring the roses nearer, let
the wine bedabble their calyces like drops of dew. Music! Where are
the violins? Where is Rosetta? Leave me, all of you.

[*Exeunt* SERVANTS. LEONCE *lies on a sofa.*]

[*Enter* ROSETTA, *elegantly dressed. Music in the distance.*]

ROSETTA [*approaches seductively*]. Leonce.

LEONCE. Rosetta.

ROSETTA. Leonce.

LEONCE. Rosetta.

ROSETTA. Your lips are weary. From kissing?

LEONCE. From yawning.

ROSETTA. Oh.

LEONCE. Rosetta, I have such hard work . . .

ROSETTA. Yes?

LEONCE. Doing nothing.

ROSETTA. Nothing but making love?

LEONCE. Hard work indeed.

ROSETTA [*offended*]. Leonce!

LEONCE. Or an occupation.

ROSETTA. Or lack of one.

LEONCE. Right as usual. You're a clever girl; I'm always telling people how clever you are.

ROSETTA. Then you love me because you are bored?

LEONCE. No, I am bored because I love you. But I love my boredom and you equally. You are one and the same thing. *O dolce far niente*! I dream of your eyes as of deep and secret springs. The caress of your lips makes me drowsy like the murmur of waves.

[*He embraces her.*]

Come, dear ennui, your kisses are a voluptuous yawn, your footsteps an elegant hiatus.

ROSETTA. Then you do love me, Leonce?

LEONCE. Why not?

ROSETTA. And for ever?

LEONCE. For ever is a long time. If I love you another five thousand years and seven months, will that do? Granted it's rather less than eternity, but it's a good length of time and we can take our time at loving one another.

ROSETTA. Or time can take our love from us.

LEONCE. Or our love can take time. Dance, Rosetta, dance. Let time run to the rhythm of your dainty feet.

ROSETTA. I'd sooner my feet took me right out of time.

[*She dances and sings.*]

> My weary feet, now you must dance
> In shoes of red,
> Though you would rather rest in peace
> On your death bed.
>
> My burning cheeks, now you must glow
> With wild caresses,
> Though you would rather bloom as pale
> As two white roses.
>
> My tired eyes, which now must shine
> In candle light,
> Would rather sleep their pain away
> In darkest night.

LEONCE [*dreaming to himself*]. Oh, a dying love is better than a living one. I'm a Roman; for the final course of my exquisite banquet golden fish die in a blaze of colour.[1] How the red fades from her cheek, how softly her eye is dimmed. How gently her limbs rise and fall. *Addio, addio*, my darling. I shall love your corpse.

[ROSETTA *goes up to him again.*]

Tears, Rosetta? It's a rare Epicureanism to be able to weep. Stand in the sun and let the precious drops crystallize. They'll turn into magnificent diamonds. You can have a necklace made of them.

ROSETTA. They're diamonds already. They cut my eyes. Oh, Leonce!

[*Tries to embrace him.*]

LEONCE. Be careful of my head; I've laid out my love's corpse in it. Look through the windows, I mean my eyes—can you see how dead the poor thing is? Can you see the two white roses on its cheeks and the two red ones on its breast? Don't nudge me; an arm might break off, and that would be a pity. I must carry my head straight on my shoulders, like a mourning woman with the coffin of a child.

---

[1] Compare *Danton's Death*, IV. v, p. 67.

ROSETTA [*laughing*]. Silly!

LEONCE. Rosetta! [ROSETTA *makes a face.*] Thank God.

> [*He puts his hands over his eyes.*]

ROSETTA [*frightened*]. Look at me, Leonce.

LEONCE. Not for the world.

ROSETTA. Just a glance.

LEONCE. Not one. What are you trying to do? The smallest thing would bring my love to life again. I'm glad to have buried it, I shall keep my impression of it.

ROSETTA [*goes sadly and slowly away, singing*].

> Poor little waif am I,
> Frightened, and all alone.
> Sweet sorrow, come:
> Will you not see me home?

> [*Exit.*]

LEONCE [*alone*]. A strange thing, love. You lie for a year in waking sleep; then one fine day you wake up, drink a glass of water, put your clothes on, run your hand over your forehead—and start to think. Start to think. How many women does a man need to sing the whole gamut of love? One can scarcely produce a single note. Why is our hazy atmosphere a prism that refracts the white light of love into a rainbow?

> [*He drinks.*]

What bottle holds the wine which shall make me drunk today? Will I even get that far? I feel like a man sitting under a vacuum pump—the air is so thin and sharp that it freezes me. It's like skating in nankeen trousers. Gentlemen, do you know what made Nero and Caligula what they were? I do.—Come, Leonce, a soliloquy. I'll listen. My life yawns at me like a great white sheet of paper; I'm supposed to write it full, but I can't squeeze out a single letter. My head is an empty ballroom: a few withered roses and crumpled ribbons on the floor, cracked violins in the corner, and the last dancers have taken their masks off and are looking at each other with weary eyes. I turn myself inside out twenty-four times a day, like a glove. Oh, I know myself: I know what I shall be thinking and dreaming of a quarter of an hour, a week, a year from now. God, what crime have I committed that you should make me repeat my lesson so often, like a dunce at school? [*He applauds.*] It does me good to call to myself occasionally. Leonce! Leonce!

[VALERIO *comes out from under a table.*]

VALERIO. Your Highness would seem to be well on the way to becoming a perfect head-case.

LEONCE. Yes, examined in the cold light of day, it would seem so.

VALERIO. A moment, and we'll discuss the matter further. I must just finish this piece of roast I filched from the kitchen and this wine I stole from your table. I'll be right with you.

LEONCE. How he smacks his chops! He calls up idyllic notions: I could start again with the simple things, I could eat cheese, drink beer, smoke tobacco. Get on with it, but don't snuffle so. And don't clash your tusks.

VALERIO. Most worthy Adonis, do you fear for your thighs? Set your mind at rest. I'm neither a broom-maker nor a schoolmaster. I need no twigs for birches.

LEONCE. You don't owe me anything.

VALERIO. I wish I could say the same for your lordship.

LEONCE. I owe you a thrashing, you mean. Are you so concerned for your education?

VALERIO. Procreation is easier to come by than education, heaven knows. It's all very sad—coming into the world means coming into woe. What labour I've known since my mother was in labour! What good have I received since being conceived?

LEONCE. Your conception will earn you a warm reception. Express yourself more agreeably, unless you want to be disagreeably impressed.

VALERIO. When my mother sailed round the Cape of Good Hope—

LEONCE. And your father was shipwrecked on Cape Horn—

VALERIO. Correct, for he was a night-watchman. But he didn't put the horn to his lips as often as the fathers of princes put horns to their foreheads.

LEONCE. The fellow's impertinence is divine. I feel the need to come into closer contact with it. I have a passionate desire to cudgel you.

VALERIO. That's a compelling argument and a striking answer.

LEONCE [*making for him*]. Your answer's more struck than striking, because you're going to be struck for it.

[VALERIO *runs away*. LEONCE *trips and falls*.]

VALERIO. Your argument remains to be proved, because it's tripped over its own fundamentals and they haven't even been established. Your calves, sir, are highly improbable, your thighs a figment.

[*Enter the* PRIVY COUNCIL. LEONCE *remains sitting on the floor*.]

LORD PRESIDENT. Pardon me, Your Highness . . .

LEONCE. As I pardon myself, for I do pardon my affability in listening to you. Gentlemen, won't you take a seat? What faces they make when they hear the word 'seat'. Don't be embarrassed. Lie on the ground. It's the last position you'll ever hold, but it brings nothing in—except for the gravedigger.

LORD PRESIDENT [*twisting his fingers with embarrassment*]. If Your Highness would be kind enough to—

LEONCE. Don't twist your fingers like that, or I'll do you an injury.

LORD PRESIDENT [*twisting his fingers all the more*]. To give his gracious consent regarding—

LEONCE. For God's sake put your hands in your pockets, or sit on them. The man's beside himself. Pull yourself together.

VALERIO. Never interrupt a child pissing. You'll give him a blockage.

LEONCE. Calm yourself, man. Think of your family. Think of the state. If you can't get the words out you'll have a stroke.

LORD PRESIDENT [*producing a paper*]. Permit me, Your Highness . . .

LEONCE. By Jove, he can read! Now then—

LORD PRESIDENT. Your royal father wishes to inform you that the long-awaited arrival of Your Highness's affianced bride, her Serene Highness Princess Lena of the kingdom of Pee, is to be expected tomorrow morning.

LEONCE. If my bride has been long awaited, I shall yield to her wishes and let her wait a little longer. I saw her in a dream last night. She had a pair of eyes so big that my Rosetta's dancing pumps would have made brows for them. There were no dimples on her cheeks, only gullies to drain off laughter. I believe in dreams. Do you dream sometimes, my Lord President? Do you have premonitions?

VALERIO. Of course he does, the night before the roast burns, a capon dies, or Your Royal Highness has the colic.

LEONCE. Apropos, weren't you trying to say something? Unburden yourself.

LORD PRESIDENT. On the nuptial day the Most High Will purposes to resign its sublime intentions and place them in Your Highness's hands.

LEONCE. Inform the Most High Will that I shall do everything except that which I shall leave undone—which however won't be as much as it would be if it were as much again. Pardon me, gentlemen, if I don't accompany you. I have as it happens a burning desire to sit down, but my grace and favour towards you is so great that I can scarcely measure it with the span of my legs. [*He spreads his legs.*] My Lord President, please measure it and remind me of the figure later. Valerio, accompany these gentlemen.

VALERIO. On the piano? Or shall I hang a cowbell round their necks and lead them off on all fours?

LEONCE. Fellow, you're nothing but a bad pun. You have neither father nor mother. The five vowels begot you upon each other.

VALERIO. And you, Prince, are a book without words—nothing but think-dots. Come now, gentlemen.—You know, there's something sad about the word 'come'. For an income you must steal, to come up in the world you must be hanged, and the outcome in either case is the grave. If nothing will come into your head your wits come short—that is coming about with me now and with you before your mouths come open. Gentlemen, you've had your come-uppance, so come away.

[*Exeunt* PRIVY COUNCIL *and* VALERIO.]

LEONCE [*alone*]. How vilely I played the cavalier with those poor devils! But then there's a certain pleasure in vileness. Hm. Marriage. That is to drink a well dry. O Shandy, old Shandy, who shall give me your timepiece![1]

[VALERIO *returns.*]

Did you hear, Valerio?

VALERIO. So you're to be king. How amusing. You can drive around all day and make people wear out their hats with lifting them; you can turn regular citizens into regular soldiers—that's the natural order of things; you can promote black frock-coats and white neckerchiefs to civil servants; and when you die all the shiny buttons will turn blue-mouldy and the bellropes snap like string from tolling. Won't that be delightful?

LEONCE. Valerio, there must be something else to do. Advise me.

VALERIO. Oh, learning, learning. We shall become philosophers. *A priori* or *a posteriori?*

LEONCE. *A priori* I'd have to learn from my father. And *a posteriori* every story starts like an old fairy-tale: Once upon a time.

VALERIO. Then let's be heroes.

[*Marches up and down imitating trumpet and drum.*]

Rum, tum. Rum-tum-tum!

LEONCE. But heroism stinks of liquor and catches hospital fever and depends on lieutenants and recruits. Away with your Napoleonic illusions!

VALERIO. Then let's be geniuses.

LEONCE. The nightingale of poesy sings all day above our heads, but the best of it goes to the devil until we tear its feathers out and dip them in paint or ink.

VALERIO. Then let's become useful members of society.

LEONCE. I'd sooner hand in my resignation from the human race.

VALERIO. Then let's go to the devil.

[1] Tristram Shandy's father, in Sterne's novel, wound up his clock on the first Sunday of every month to remind him to make love to his wife.

LEONCE. Oh, the devil's only there for the sake of contrast, to let us know there's something in the idea of heaven after all. [*Jumping up.*] I've got it, Valerio. Don't you feel a wind from the south? Don't you feel the hot blue air swirling around you, the light flashing from sun-gold earth, salt holy sea, and marble pillars and statues? Great Pan is asleep and brazen figures are dreaming in the shade, over-looking the murmuring sea—dreaming of the old enchanter Virgil, of tarantella and tambourine and mad dark nights full of masks, torches, and guitars. A beggar, Valerio, a *lazzarone*! We'll go to Italy.

SCENE IV
A garden.

PRINCESS LENA *in her bridal dress, the* GOVERNESS.

LENA. Now it's come. Now. I never thought about it, but time passed, and now, suddenly, the day has risen up before me. The garland is in my hair—and those bells, those bells! [*She leans back and closes her eyes.*] I wish the grass grew over me and bees hummed above my head. But I'm dressed in white, with rosemary in my hair. Isn't there an old song:

> In the churchyard I would lie,
> Lulla, lulla, lullabye.

GOVERNESS. Poor child. How pale you are in the glitter of your jewels.

LENA. Oh God, I could love someone—why should I not? We go through life so lonely, looking for a hand to hold until death pulls both hands apart and folds them on their individual breasts. But why drive a nail through two hands that never sought each other out? What has my poor hand done? [*She pulls a ring from her finger.*] This ring stings me like an adder.

GOVERNESS. But they say he's a real Don Carlos . . .

LENA. He's a man—

GOVERNESS. Well?

LENA. Whom one doesn't love. [*She stands up.*] Fie! I'm ashamed, you see. Tomorrow all my gloss and fragrance will have been brushed off. Am I then like the defenceless pool whose quiet depths have to mirror whatever image bends over them? The flowers open and shut their cups to morning sun and evening breeze as they choose. Is a king's daughter less than a flower?

GOVERNESS [*weeping*]. My poor angel, poor lamb to the slaughter!

LENA. Yes, and the priest is already raising the knife. Dear God, is it true then that we must redeem ourselves with our suffering? Is it true that the world is a crucified saviour, the sun his crown of thorns and the stars the nails in his feet, the spear in his side?

GOVERNESS. My child, my child! I can't bear to see you like this. It can't go on, it will kill you.—Maybe, who knows . . . I've got an idea. We shall see. Come!

[*She leads the Princess away.*]

ACT TWO

And then I heard a voice ring out
Deep down in me,
Which in a moment rapt away
My memory.

ADALBERT VON CHAMISSO

SCENE I

Open country, with an inn in the background.

[*Enter* LEONCE *and* VALERIO. VALERIO *with a bundle.*]

VALERIO [*panting*]. On my honour, Prince, the world is a monstrous great building.

LEONCE. No, no. It's a hall of mirrors, so narrow I hardly dare stretch my arms out for fear of smashing them. The lovely figures would lie in splinters at my feet and I'd be left standing in front of the bare naked walls.

VALERIO. I'm lost.

LEONCE. That's a loss to nobody but the man who finds you.

VALERIO. I'm going to stop a moment in my shadow's shadow.

LEONCE. The sun's converting you into hot air. Do you see that pretty cloud? It's about a quarter of you. It's looking down at your grosser stuff with a sense of self-satisfaction.

VALERIO. It wouldn't do any harm if it were precipitated on your head drop by drop. What a priceless thought: we've walked full tilt through a dozen principalities, six grand duchies, and a couple of kingdoms, all in half a day—and why? Because you're to be king and marry a beautiful princess. How can you bear to live? I don't understand your resignation. I don't understand why you haven't taken arsenic, climbed a church steeple, stood on the parapet, and blown your brains out. Just to make sure.

LEONCE. You're forgetting my ideals, Valerio. There's an ideal woman in my mind; I must keep looking for her. She is exquisitely beautiful and exquisitely stupid. Her beauty has the touching helplessness of a new-born babe. What a delightful contrast: those divinely vacuous eyes, that gorgeously vapid mouth, that Grecian profile worthy of a sheep, spiritual death in a mindless body.

VALERIO. Damnation, we've reached the frontier again. This country is like an onion—nothing but skins. Or like a set of Chinese boxes: all the bigger ones have inside them is other boxes, and the smallest one has nothing at all. [*He throws down his bundle.*] Is this bundle to be my tombstone? Prince, I am turning philosopher: observe my paradigm of life. I lug this bundle with aching feet through frost and broiling sun, just so that I can put on a clean shirt in the evening. But when the evening finally comes my brow is furrowed, my cheek sunken, my eye dim. I have only just time to put my shirt on— as a shroud. Wouldn't it have been more sensible to take the bundle off its stick and auction the contents at the nearest inn? I could have got drunk and slept in the shade instead of sweating and giving myself corns. And now, Prince, for the practical application: for modesty's sake let's clothe the inner man and give our guts coats and trousers.

[*They go towards the inn.*]

My dear bundle, how sweet you smell! What odours of wine and roast! My breeches take root and flourish like the vine! The grapes dangle into my mouth in great heavy bunches, and the new wine ferments in the press.

[*Exeunt.*]

[*Enter* PRINCESS LENA *and the* GOVERNESS.]

GOVERNESS. The day must be bewitched. It's ages since we ran away; the sun refuses to set.

LENA. Oh no, dear governess. The flowers I picked in the garden are hardly wilted yet.

GOVERNESS. Where shall we sleep? We haven't come across a single place. Not a convent, not a hermit's cell, not a shepherd's hut.

LENA. It was all quite different in our dreams, in the books we read among the myrtles and oleanders, behind our garden wall.

GOVERNESS. The world is hideous. We must give up all idea of meeting a wandering prince.

LENA. No, it's beautiful—and so wide, so boundlessly wide. I should like to go on for ever, day and night. Nothing stirs. A shimmer of red flowers plays on the meadows and the distant mountains lie on the earth like resting clouds.

GOVERNESS. Sweet Jesus, what will they say? Yet the whole thing is so feminine and refined. It's a renunciation, like the flight of Saint Odile. But we must look for shelter, evening is coming on.

LENA. Yes, and the plants are closing their leaves in sleep, and the sunbeams swinging on the grassblades like weary dragonflies.

SCENE II
The inn garden, on a hillock overlooking a river; panoramic view.

VALERIO, LEONCE.

VALERIO. Now, Prince, didn't your trousers yield an exquisite tipple? Your boots fairly ran down your throat.

LEONCE. Look at the old trees, the hedges, the flowers. They all have charming and mysterious stories to tell. Do you see those friendly-faced old men under the arbour at the inn door? They sit there holding each other's hands, frightened because they are so old and the world so young. I'm young too, Valerio; it's the world which is old. I'm sometimes anxious about myself. I could sit in a corner and weep salt tears from self-pity.

VALERIO [*gives him a glass*]. Take this diving bell and plunge into the sea of wine till the bubbles burst above you. Look, there are elves floating in its bouquet, shod with gold and clashing cymbals.

LEONCE [*jumping up*]. Come on, Valerio, we must do something. Let's busy ourselves with profound thoughts, let's investigate the problem of why a chair will stand on three legs but not on two. Come on, we'll dissect ants and count the filaments of flowers. I'll work up some sort of princely hobby yet. I'll find a baby's rattle that will stay in my hand till my fingers make wool-flocks and pluck at the blanket. I've still a certain dose of enthusiasm to swallow, but when it's all nicely warmed up I take a devilish time to find a spoon and then it goes stale.

VALERIO. *Ergo bibamus*! Do you see this bottle? It's neither a mistress nor an idea. No birth pangs for it; it's neither boring nor unfaithful, it's the same from the first drop to the last. Break the seal and all the dreams asleep inside bubble out at you.

LEONCE. Oh God, I'll spend half my life in prayer if you but grant me a straw: I'll ride it like a magnificent charger till I lie on straw myself. What a weird evening! Down here everything is silent, but up there the clouds change and pass, the sunshine comes and goes. What strange shapes hurry past—do you see those long white shadows with skeleton legs and bats' wings? Everything so swift and confused, yet down here not a leaf stirs, not a blade of grass. The earth is cowering like a frightened child, and ghosts are walking about its cradle.

VALERIO. I don't know what you want. Speaking for myself, I'm quite comfortable thank you. The sun looks like an inn sign; you can read the inscription on the blazing clouds above it: Inn of the Golden Sun. The land and water below are a table with wine spilled on it, and we lie there like playing cards; God and the devil are having a game with us to pass the time. You're the king and I'm the knave; all we need's a queen, a nice queen with a great gingerbread heart on her corsage and a huge tulip to dip her girlish nose in—

[*Enter the* GOVERNESS *and* LENA.]

—and by heaven, there she is! Only she hasn't a tulip but a pinch of snuff, and her nose is more of an elephant's trunk. [*To the* GOVERNESS] Most worthy dame, why do you stride out so fast that you reveal your erstwhile calves up to your respectable garters?

GOVERNESS [*stops in high dudgeon*]. And why, most honoured sir, do you open your mouth so wide that you make a gap in the scenery?

VALERIO. Honoured madam, to prevent you banging your nose against the horizon. A nose like that is as the tower of Lebanon which looketh towards Damascus.

LENA [*to the* GOVERNESS]. Is the way so long then?

LEONCE [*daydreaming*]. All ways are long. The death-watch beetle ticks slowly in our bosoms, each drop of blood measures out its time, and life is a lingering fever. For weary feet all ways are long.

LENA [*listens, anxiously pondering*]. For weary eyes every light is too bright, for weary lips every breath too heavy. [*Smiling.*] And for weary ears every word is one too many.

[*Goes into the inn with the* GOVERNESS.]

LEONCE. My dear Valerio, might I not say with Hamlet: 'Would not this, sir, and a forest of feathers—if the rest of my fortunes turn Turk with me—with two Provincial roses on my rased shoes, get me a fellowship in a cry of players?' I believe I spoke with great sadness. Thank God I'm beginning to be brought to bed of my melancholy! The air's no longer so bright and cold, the sky comes down around me, lurid and thick, and heavy raindrops fall. Oh that voice! 'Is the way so long then?' The world is full of voices and they all seem to speak of different things. But this is one I understand. It lays its hand on me like the spirit of God moving upon the face of the waters before light was. What a roaring of the deep, what genesis in me, how her voice pours through space! 'Is the way so long then?'

[*Exit.*]

VALERIO. No, it's not too long to the madhouse. It's easy to find; I know all the highways and byways. I can see he's taken the main road; there he is, on an icy winter's day, standing in the long shadows of the leafless trees with his hat under his arm, fanning his face with his handkerchief. The man's mad!

SCENE III

A room.

LENA, *the* GOVERNESS.

GOVERNESS. Don't think about him.

LENA. He was so old, for all his blond curls. Spring on his cheeks and winter in his heart. It's sad. The weary body can always find a pillow, but where can the tired spirit rest? I've just had a terrible thought: there are men who are unhappy—yes, incurable, merely because they are. [*She stands up.*]

GOVERNESS. Where are you going, my child?

LENA. Down to the garden.

GOVERNESS. But—

LENA. But, dear governess? You know me; I should have been put in a flowerpot when I was a child. I need dew and night air, like the flowers. Can you hear the sounds evening makes? Crickets are singing the day to sleep, and violets making it drowsy with their scent. I can't stay indoors. The walls are crowding in on me.

SCENE IV
The garden. Moonlight.

LENA, *sitting on the grass.* [VALERIO *a little way off.*]

VALERIO. Nature's all very fine but it would be even finer if there weren't so many midges and the inn beds were a little cleaner and the death-watch beetles didn't tick in the walls so. Inside, snoring men; out here, croaking frogs. Inside, the chirp of crickets on the hearth; out here, grasshoppers. Earth, I have made a down-to-earth decision.

[*Lies down on the grass.*]

[LEONCE *enters.*]

LEONCE. Such a night, balmy as the first that fell in Eden.

[*Sees* LENA *and creeps up to her.*]

LENA [*to herself*]. The hedge-sparrow twittered in its sleep. The night is sleeping sounder; its cheeks grow paler, its breath quieter. The moon is asleep too like a child: its golden hair has fallen about its charming face. Oh, it's dead, not asleep! The angel of death lies on its dark pillow; the stars are burning round it like candles. Poor child, so sad, dead and alone.

LEONCE. Stand up in your white dress. Follow the corpse through the night, singing its requiem.

LENA. Who is there?

LEONCE. A dream.

LENA. Dreams are blessed.

LEONCE. Then dream yourself into a state of blessedness and let me be your blessed dream.

LENA. The most blessed dream is death.

LEONCE. Then let me be your angel of death. Let my lips touch your eyes like his wings. [*He kisses her.*] Beautiful corpse, you lie so lovely on the black pall of night. You make nature abhor life and fall in love with death.

LENA. No, leave me!

[*She jumps up and runs away.*]

LEONCE. It is too much! My whole existence summed up in that one moment. Now die; more is impossible. Creation, freshly breathing, radiantly beautiful, struggles towards me out of chaos. The earth is a dark gold chalice; light sparkles in it and overflows; stars come bubbling up. This one drop of bliss makes me a precious vessel. Sacred cup, I cast you down!

[*Prepares to throw himself into the river.*]

VALERIO [*jumps up and catches hold of him*]. Serene Highness, stop.

LEONCE. Leave me.

VALERIO. I'll leave you when you leave off. Leave the river to its own devices.

LEONCE. Blockhead.

VALERIO. Haven't you got over this officer's mess nonsense, throwing your glass out the window when you've drunk your sweetheart's health?

LEONCE. I almost believe you're right.

VALERIO. Console yourself. If you can't sleep under the grass tonight, try sleeping on top of it. It would be just as suicidal to go to bed; you lie on your straw like a dead man, but the fleas bite you like a living one.

LEONCE. Very well. [*He lies on the grass.*] You've robbed me of a first-class suicide. I'll never get a better chance in my life again, and the weather so perfect. I'm not in the mood any more. The fool has ruined everything with his yellow waistcoat and sky-blue breeches. Heaven grant me a vulgar, healthy sleep.

VALERIO. Amen. I've saved a human life; my good conscience will keep me warm.

LEONCE. I wish you joy of it, Valerio.

ACT THREE

SCENE I
A garden.

LEONCE, VALERIO.

VALERIO. Marry? Since when has Your Highness accepted the idea of forever?

LEONCE. Don't you know, Valerio, that even the most insignificant of men is so important that a lifetime is far too short to love him in? Some people think that nothing is so fine and holy but they could make it more so. Well, good luck to them. There's a certain pleasure to be had from that kind of arrogance. Why should I begrudge it them?

VALERIO. Very humane. Very philobestial. But does she know who you are?

LEONCE. She only knows she loves me.

VALERIO. And does Your Highness know who she is?

LEONCE. Blockhead. Ask the carnation and the drop of dew what their names are.

VALERIO. Well, she must be somebody, if that doesn't sound too indelicate, too much like a police notice. But how can we bring it about? Hm. Prince, will you make me Prime Minister if I link you to your nameless and inexpressible lady—this very day, and with your father's blessing? Do you promise?

LEONCE. I promise.

VALERIO. Valerio the starveling commends himself to His Excellency the Prime Minister, Valerio von Valeriental. 'What does the fellow want? Be off, you rascal. I know thee not!'

[*He runs off;* LEONCE *follows him.*]

Scene II

Open space before King Peter's palace.

MAGISTRATE, SCHOOLMASTER, PEASANTS *in their Sunday best,
holding fir branches.*

MAGISTRATE. How are your people bearing up, schoolmaster?

SCHOOLMASTER. They're bearing their misfortunes so manfully that
they've learnt to bear with their fellow-men. They keep pouring
spirits down their throats, otherwise they couldn't bear the heat.
Courage, good people. Hold your fir branches straight up in front
of you; then people will think you're a forest, your noses straw-
berries, your cocked hats antlers, and your buckskin trousers moon-
shine. And remember, the man at the back is to keep running round
to the front to make it look as if your numbers were raised to the
power of two. . . .

MAGISTRATE. And, schoolmaster, you stand guarantor for their sobriety.

SCHOOLMASTER. Certainly. I'm so sober I can hardly stand myself.

MAGISTRATE. Listen to me, good people. The programme says: 'All
subjects will voluntarily line the road, properly dressed, well-fed,
and with contented faces.' So no nonsense, please.

SCHOOLMASTER. Stand up straight. Don't scratch behind your ears or
blow your nose with your fingers while the royal pair drive past.
And whip up a proper enthusiasm or we shall have to whip it up for
you. Think of the favour conferred on you: you have been placed
downwind of the kitchens, so you won't die without having smelt
roast beef. Do you know your lesson? Eh? Vi!

PEASANTS. Vi!

SCHOOLMASTER. Vat!

PEASANTS. Vat!

SCHOOLMASTER. Vivat!

PEASANTS. Vivat!

SCHOOLMASTER. Observe, your worship. Intelligence is on the increase.
Latin; think of that. And tonight we're giving a fancy dress ball:
the holes in our clothes will make do for fairy lights and we'll
beat each other's faces black and blue for cockades.

Scene III
A great hall.

LADIES *and* GENTLEMEN, *splendidly dressed, standing in studied groups. In the foreground, the* MASTER OF THE REVELS *with* SERVANTS.

MASTER OF THE REVELS. What a state of affairs! Everything's going to pot. The roasts are burning and the congratulations going stale. The stand-up collars are lying down as sadly as pigs' ears. The peasants' nails and beards are growing again. The soldiers' pigtails are coming undone. And the twelve bridesmaids would rather be lying down than standing up.

1 SERVANT. They look like worn-out angora rabbits in their white dresses, and the court poet is grunting round them like a distressed guinea pig. The officers of the guard have gone limp and the ladies-in-waiting are standing there making distilled water; the salt is crystallizing on their necklaces.

2 SERVANT. At least they're taking things easy. Nobody could say they've too much on their backs. They may not be open-hearted, but they're certainly bare-breasted.

MASTER OF THE REVELS. They'd make excellent maps of the Turkish Empire. You can see the Dardanelles and the Sea of Marmora. Now be off, you rascals. To the windows! His Majesty is coming.

[*Enter* KING PETER *with the* PRIVY COUNCIL.]

KING PETER. So the Princess has vanished too. Still no trace of our beloved Crown Prince? Are my orders being obeyed? Are the frontiers being watched?

MASTER OF THE REVELS. Yes, Your Majesty. The view from these windows permits the strictest surveillance. [*To the* FIRST SERVANT] What do you see?

1 SERVANT. A dog has just run through the kingdom looking for its master.

MASTER OF THE REVELS [*to another* SERVANT]. And you?

2 SERVANT. Someone's gone for a walk along the northern frontier, but it's not the Prince. I'd recognize him from here.

MASTER OF THE REVELS. And you?

3 SERVANT. Nothing, beg pardon.

MASTER OF THE REVELS. That's not much. What about you?

4 SERVANT. Nothing either.

MASTER OF THE REVELS. That's no better.

KING PETER. But, gentlemen of the Council, did we not resolve that my Royal Majesty would rejoice today, and that the wedding would be celebrated? Was not that our firm resolve?

LORD PRESIDENT. Yes, Your Majesty. It is recorded in the minutes.

KING PETER. And would I not be compromised if I failed to carry out my decision?

LORD PRESIDENT. If indeed it were possible for Your Majesty to be compromised this would be a case in which such a compromise might occur.

KING PETER. Have I not given my royal word?—Yes, I shall immediately put my decision into effect. I shall rejoice. [*Rubs his hands.*] I am exceptionally joyful.

LORD PRESIDENT. We share Your Majesty's sentiments, insofar as it is fit and proper for subjects so to do.

KING PETER. I'm so joyful I don't know what to do. My chamberlains will have new red coats. I shall promote a few cadets to the rank of lieutenant. I shall permit my subjects . . . But what about the wedding? Doesn't the other half of the resolution say that the wedding is to be celebrated?

LORD PRESIDENT. Yes, Your Majesty.

KING PETER. What if the Prince and Princess don't come?

LORD PRESIDENT. Well, if the Prince doesn't come, and the Princess doesn't come either, then . . . then . . .

KING PETER. Then what?

LORD PRESIDENT. Then they can't be married.

KING PETER. Stop. Is that a logical conclusion? If the Prince, then they can't . . . Quite right. But my word, my royal word!

LORD PRESIDENT. Your Majesty, take comfort in the conduct of other Majesties. A sovereign's word is a thing . . . a thing that means nothing at all.

KING PETER [*to the* SERVANTS]. Do you see anything yet?

SERVANTS. Nothing, Your Majesty.

KING PETER. And I had resolved to have such rejoicings! I was going to start on the stroke of twelve and carry on for precisely twelve hours. Now I feel quite melancholy.

LORD PRESIDENT. All subjects are commanded to share the feelings of His Majesty.

MASTER OF THE REVELS. In the interests of decency however subjects not in possession of a handkerchief are forbidden to weep.

I SERVANT. Wait! I can see something. A kind of protrusion, like a nose: the rest of it hasn't crossed the border yet. Then there's another man, and two persons not of the same sex.

MASTER OF THE REVELS. Which way are they going?

I SERVANT. This way. They are approaching the palace. They're here.

[*Enter* VALERIO, LEONCE, *the* GOVERNESS, *and* LENA, *masked*.]

KING PETER. Who are you?

VALERIO. How should I know? [*He slowly takes off a series of masks, one after another*.] Am I this? Or this? Or this? I'm getting frightened; I shall peel myself away to nothing.

KING PETER [*at a loss*]. But you must be somebody!

VALERIO. As Your Majesty commands. But, gentlemen, turn the mirrors back to front, cover up your shiny buttons and don't look at me: I don't want to see myself reflected in your eyes. Otherwise I really shan't know who I am.

KING PETER. The fellow has confused me. I'm highly perplexed. I'm on the point of despair.

VALERIO. But as a matter of fact I came to announce to this honourable and distinguished company that the two world-famous automata have arrived. I might even say that I'm the third and most remarkable of the pair, only I don't know who I am—which by the way shouldn't surprise anybody, as I haven't the remotest idea what I'm talking about, indeed I don't even know that I don't know, which makes it highly probable that somebody else is doing the talking and I'm only an arrangement of pipes and bellows. [*In a rasping barker's voice*] My lords and ladies, you see before you two persons of different sexes, one male and one female, one little lady and one little gentleman. All a mechanical trick, nothing but pasteboard and watch-springs. Each has a superfine ruby-mounted spring under the little toenail of the right foot. Press it ever so gently and the mechanism will run for a good fifty years. These objects are so consummately made that unless you knew they were only pasteboard you couldn't distinguish them from real human beings. You might even accept them in society. They are well born: they speak high German. They are also moral: they get up, have luncheon, and retire to bed by the clock. They have excellent digestions, which proves that their consciences are clear. They have a keen sense of propriety, the lady having no word for the concept of drawers and the gentleman being incapable of going upstairs behind a lady or downstairs in front of her. They are very cultivated: the lady can sing all the latest opera tunes and the gentleman wears cuffs. Watch carefully, ladies and gentlemen; they are at a highly interesting stage of development. The mechanism of love has just begun to operate: the gentleman has already carried the lady's shawl a few times, and the lady has averted her eyes and gazed mutely at heaven. Both have already whispered: Faith, Hope, Love. They appear to be in agreement and all that's missing is one little word: Amen.

KING PETER [*putting his finger to his nose*]. In effigy! My Lord President, if you hang a man in effigy isn't that just as good as if you hanged him in earnest?

LORD PRESIDENT. Pardon me, Your Majesty, it is much better; because he doesn't come to any harm yet he is hanged just the same.

KING PETER. I have it. We shall celebrate the wedding in effigy. [*Pointing to* LEONCE *and* LENA.] Here is your princess, and here is your prince. I shall carry out my resolution, I shall rejoice. Ring the bells. Get your congratulations ready. Hurry up, chaplain!

[*The* COURT CHAPLAIN *steps forward, clears his throat and looks upwards a few times.*]

VALERIO. Begin. Pox, leave thy damnable faces and begin. Come!

COURT CHAPLAIN [*greatly confused*]. Dearly beloved, we . . . er . . .

VALERIO. Forasmuch as and insofar—

COURT CHAPLAIN. For indeed—

VALERIO. Before the world was made . . .

COURT CHAPLAIN. In that—

VALERIO. Almighty God was bored.

KING PETER. Make it short, my good man.

COURT CHAPLAIN [*collecting his wits*]. If it please Your Highness Prince Leonce of the kingdom of Po, if it please Your Highness Princess Lena of the kingdom of Pee, if it please Your Highnesses mutually and conjointly to take one another for man and wife, then indicate the same with a loud and clear Yes.

LENA and LEONCE. Yes.

COURT CHAPLAIN. Then I say Amen.

VALERIO. Well done, short and to the point. Thus God created man and woman, and all the creatures of Eden stood around.

[LEONCE *takes off his mask.*]

ALL. The Prince!

KING PETER. The Prince. My son. I'm lost, I've been tricked. [*Goes up to* LENA.] Who is this person? I declare everything null and void.

GOVERNESS [*taking off* LENA's *mask, triumphantly*]. The Princess!

LEONCE. Lena?

LENA. Leonce?

LEONCE. Oh, Lena, I think I escaped into paradise.

LENA. I've been tricked.

LEONCE. So have I.

LENA. Chance.

LEONCE. Providence.

VALERIO. I really can't help laughing. It falls out that Your Highnesses fall to each other's lot. It's well that it falls out so, and I only hope you don't fall out with each other.

GOVERNESS. To think I should live to see the day. A wandering prince! Now I can die happy.

KING PETER. My children, I am moved. I am so moved I can hardly speak. I am the happiest of men. My son, I solemnly place the government in your hands. Now I can think in peace. You will relinquish these wise counsellors [*he points to the Council of State*] to me; they will support me in my endeavours. Come, gentlemen, we must devote ourselves to uninterrupted thought. [*Going out with the* PRIVY COUNCIL.] This fellow confused me a moment ago. I must think my way out of it.

[*Exeunt.*]

LEONCE [*to those who remain*]. Gentlemen, my consort and I deeply regret that you have been kept waiting so long for our sake. Your condition is so pitiful that no power on earth would make us try your constancy further. Go home now, but don't forget your speeches, sermons, and verses: tomorrow, in all tranquillity, we shall go through the whole farce again. Farewell.

[*Exeunt omnes.* LEONCE, LENA, VALERIO, *and the* GOVERNESS *remain.*]

LEONCE. Now, Lena, you see how many toys and dolls we have in our pockets. What shall we do with them? Shall we give them swords and moustaches? Shall we dress them up in tailcoats and watch through a magnifying glass while they play at Lilliputian politics and diplomacy? Or would you like a barrel-organ with white mice scampering on it, striking aesthetic poses? Shall we build a theatre?

[LENA *leans against him and shakes her head.*]

But I know what you really want. We'll smash all clocks, proscribe all calendars, and reckon hours and months according to nature's timepiece, by blossom-time and fruit-bearing. And then we'll surround our little kingdom with burning-glasses to banish winter, and in summer we'll brew up a climate like Capri and Ischia. We'll live all the year round among roses and violets, bay leaves and orange blossom

VALERIO. And I shall be Prime Minister and a decree will be published proclaiming that all persons with calluses on their hands will be taken into custody, that working oneself sick will be an offence liable to criminal proceedings, and that any subject who boasts of earning his bread by the sweat of his brow will be declared a dangerous lunatic. And then we shall lie down in the shade and pray God for macaroni, melons, and figs, for musical voices, classical torsos, and an accommodating religion!

WOYZECK

[1836–1837]

DRAMATIS PERSONAE

WOYZECK

CAPTAIN

ANDRES

OLD MAN WITH HURDY GURDY

BARKER

DRUM MAJOR

SERGEANT

SHOWMAN

DOCTOR

JEW

KARL, THE IDIOT

LANDLORD

TWO APPRENTICES

TWO MEN

MARIE

MARGRET

GRANDMOTHER

KÄTHE

THREE GIRLS

Soldiers, students, boys and girls, etc.

At the CAPTAIN's.

CAPTAIN *sitting on a chair;* WOYZECK *shaving him.*

CAPTAIN. Not so fast, Woyzeck. One thing after another. You're making me quite dizzy. So you finish ten minutes early—what use is that to me? Think, Woyzeck, you've got a good thirty years ahead of you. Thirty years. That's three hundred and sixty months. Not to mention days, hours, and minutes! What are you going to do with all that time? Space it out, Woyzeck!

WOYZECK. Yes sir.

CAPTAIN. When I think about eternity I start worrying—about the world. Food for thought, Woyzeck, food for thought. Eternity is eternity is eternity. That's quite clear. But then again it's not eternity at all, it's the twinkling of an eye. Yes, the twinkling of an eye. Woyzeck, I shudder when I think that the earth takes a whole day to rotate. What a waste of time! And where's it going to end? Woyzeck, the very sight of a millwheel depresses me.

WOYZECK. Yes sir.

CAPTAIN. Woyzeck, you always look so worked up. A decent chap doesn't look like that, I mean a decent chap with a clear conscience. Well, say something, Woyzeck. What's the weather like today?

WOYZECK. Bad, sir. Bad. Windy.

CAPTAIN. I can feel it blustering away out there. That sort of wind affects me like a mouse. [*Slyly*] I think it's a north-southerly.

WOYZECK. Yes sir.

CAPTAIN. Ha ha ha! North-southerly. Ha ha ha! God, but he's dense. Horribly dense. [*Emotionally*] Woyzeck, you're a good chap but, [*solemnly*] Woyzeck, you've got no sense of decency. Decency is when a chap acts decently, do you follow? It's a good word. You've got a child without benefit of clergy, as our right reverend padre puts it—without benefit of clergy. It's not *my* phrase.

WOYZECK. Sir. God in heaven's not going to worry about the poor brat just because nobody said Amen before his making. Our Lord said: Suffer the little children to come unto me.

CAPTAIN. What's that? What sort of answer's that? He's got me all muddled answering like that. I—I don't mean he, I mean you. You.

WOYZECK. When you're poor like us, sir . . . It's the money, the money! If you haven't got the money . . . I mean you can't bring the likes of us into the world on decency. We're flesh and blood too. Our kind doesn't get a chance in this world or the next. If we go to heaven they'll put us to work on the thunder.

CAPTAIN. Woyzeck, you have no self-control. You are not a decent man. Flesh and blood? Why, when I'm lying by my window after a rain-shower and I see all those pretty white stockings twinkling across the street . . . damn it, Woyzeck, I feel love! I'm flesh and blood too. That's where self-control comes in, Woyzeck. The things I could waste my time on! But I say to myself: You are a decent chap, [*maudlin*] a good chap, a good chap.

WOYZECK. Oh, self-control. I'm not very strong on that, sir. You see, the likes of us just don't have any self-control. I mean, we obey nature's call. But if I were a gentleman and had a hat and a watch and a topcoat and could talk proper, then I'd have self-control all right. Must be a fine thing, self-control. But I'm a poor man.

CAPTAIN. Well said, Woyzeck. You're a good chap. But you think too much. It's wearing you out. You always look so worked up. Our little chat has got me quite excited. Off you go now—and don't run. Take it easy. Walk down the street, nice and slow.

SCENE II

Open country, with the town in the distance.

WOYZECK *and* ANDRES *cutting sticks in the bushes.*

[ANDRES *whistles.*]

WOYZECK. It's true, Andres. There's a curse on this place. Do you see that light patch on the grass over there? Where the toadstools are. That's where this head comes rolling down every night. Somebody picked it up once, thought it was a hedgehog. Three days and three nights later he was in his coffin. [*Whispering*] It was the Freemasons, Andres. Straight, it was.

ANDRES [*sings*].   A pair of hares were sitting there,
                              Nibbling the green, green grass . . .

WOYZECK. Shh. Can you hear it, Andres? There's something moving.

ANDRES.   Nibbling the green, green grass
                              Until the ground was bare.

WOYZECK. There's something moving. Behind me. Underneath me. [*Stamps on the ground.*] Listen; it's hollow. The whole bloody place is hollow. Freemasons!

ANDRES. I'm scared.

WOYZECK. Funny how silent it is. Makes you want to hold your breath. —Andres!

ANDRES. What?

WOYZECK. Say something. [*Stares around him.*] Andres, look how bright it is. It's all lit up above the town. The sky's on fire, and down there it's blaring like a brass band. It's coming up! Quick, don't look behind you.   [*Drags him into the bushes.*]

ANDRES [*after a pause*]. Woyzeck. Do you still hear it?

WOYZECK. It's silent now. Not a sound. Like the world was dead.

ANDRES. Listen, there's the drum. We've got to get back.

SCENE III
The town.

MARIE, *sitting at a window with her child on her arm*; MARGRET.

[*The Retreat passes, led by the* DRUM MAJOR.]

MARIE [*holding the child up*]. There you are, boy. Brum, brum, brum. Do you hear?

MARGRET. What a man. Built like a tree.

MARIE. The walk of him—like a lion.

[DRUM MAJOR *salutes her.*]

MARGRET. Ooh, you gave him the glad eye, neighbour. That's not like you.

MARIE [*sings*]. Oh, soldiers are such handsome lads . . .

MARGRET. There's still a gleam in your eye.

MARIE. What if there is? Take yours to Abie the pawnbroker and get them polished; if they shine properly you can sell them for buttons.

MARGRET. Hark at miss motherhood. I'm a decent girl, I am. And everybody knows you can see your way through a pair of leather breeches.

MARIE. Bitch. [*Slams the window shut.*] Come on, boy. Let them talk. You're only a whore's brat but I love your bastard's face. Brum, brum.

[*Sings*]   'What shall you do now, my pretty maid?
          You've got a baby without a dad.'
          Never you mind about me.
          All night long I'll sit and sing:
          'Rockabye, rockabye, tiny thing',
          Though nobody cares for me.

          Unsaddle your six white horses, do,
          And give them fodder fresh and new.
          Oats they won't eat for you
          Nor water drink for you,
          Nothing will do but wine, heigh-ho!
          Nothing but pure cold wine.

          [*There is a knock at the window.*]

MARIE. Who's there? Is it you, Franz? Come in.

WOYZECK. I can't. Got to go to muster.

MARIE. Have you been cutting wood for the Captain?

WOYZECK. Yes, Marie.

MARIE. What's wrong, Franz? You look in a terrible way.

WOYZECK [*mysteriously*]. It happened again, Marie. Lots of things. Doesn't the good book say: 'And behold, there was a smoke coming from the land like the smoke of an oven'?

MARIE. Oh, Franz.

WOYZECK. It followed me right to the edge of town. Something we can't grasp, something we can't understand, something that drives us mad. What will come of it?

MARIE. Franz.

WOYZECK. I've got to go. See you tonight at the fair. I've put something aside. [*He goes.*]

MARIE. The man's seeing things. Didn't even look at his own child. Thinking's driving him crazy. [*To the child*] You're keeping mum, young fellow. Are you scared? It's getting so dark; it's like you were blind. Only that street lamp shining in. I can't stand it. It gives me the creeps. [*Goes out.*]

SCENE IV
Fairground with booths. Lights. People.

[WOYZECK, MARIE *at the fair.*]

OLD MAN [*singing to a hurdy-gurdy while child dances*].

> On earth is no abiding stay.
> All men must pass away.
> That truth is known for aye.

WOYZECK. Jump to it, lad. Poor old man, poor young fellow. Joy and tribulation.

MARIE. When fools start talking sense then we're fools ourselves. It's a funny world.—No! It's a lovely world.

[*They move on to the* BARKER's *pitch.*]

BARKER [*in front of a stall, with his wife in trousers and a monkey dressed up as a man*]. Roll up, ladies and gentlemen. Examine this beast as God created him. Nothing to him, you see? Then observe the effect of art: he walks upright and has a coat and trousers. Also a sword. The monkey's a soldier—not that that's much, lowest form of animal life.—Hey! Show us your bow. Now you're a baron. Blow us a kiss. [*He plays the trumpet.*] The little blighter likes music. Gentlemen, roll up and see the little love birds and the astronomical horse. Admired by all the crowned heads of Europe. Tell you anything you like— how old you are, how many children, what illnesses you've had. The performance is about to begin. It is the *commencemong* of the *commencemong*.

WOYZECK. Want to go in?

MARIE. I don't mind. It must be nice in there. The tassels the man has. And his wife's got trousers.

[*Both off, into the booth.*]

[DRUM MAJOR, SERGEANT *passing.*]

DRUM MAJOR. Hold it. Did you see her? That's what I call a woman.

SERGEANT. Jesus! You could foal a cavalry regiment from her.

DRUM MAJOR. And breed drum majors.

SERGEANT. Look at the way she carries her head. You'd think all that black hair would weigh her down. And those eyes!

DRUM MAJOR. Like looking down a well, or a chimney. Come on. After her.

SCENE V
Inside the brightly lit booth.

[MARIE, WOYZECK, DRUM MAJOR, SERGEANT.]

MARIE. Look at the lights.

WOYZECK. Yes, Marie. Black cats with burning eyes. What a night.

SHOWMAN [*leading forward a horse*]. Show them your paces. Show them your horse sense. Put human society to shame. Gentlemen, this beast you see here with four hooves and a tail behind is a member of all the learned societies and a professor at the university. He teaches the students riding and kicking.—That's a matter of horse sense. Now show us what you can do when you use your powers of reason. Is there an ass in this learned company?

[*The horse shakes its head.*]

. . . . . . That's the power of reason. A horse of a different colour. . . . . human being in animal

. . . . *horse behaves indecently.*]

. . . . ., this animal is still in a . . . . . a lesson from him. Ask . . . . message was: Man, be . . . d slime. Would you be . . . re if you want to know . . . an't count on his fingers. . . . t explain things. He's a . . . lemen what time it is.— . . . :ch, please.

. . . *owly and majestically takes . . . a watch from his pocket.*]

. . . *umbers on to the front row.*]

SCENE VI
MARIE'*s bedroom.*

MARIE *sitting with her child on her lap and a piece of mirror in her hand.*

MARIE. The other man gave him an order and he had to go! [*Looks in the mirror.*] How they glitter. I wonder what sort of stones they are. What was it he said? Sleep, child. Shut your eyes tight.

[*Child puts its hands over its eyes.*]

Tighter. Don't move, or he'll catch you.

[*Sings*]   Polly, close the shutter tight,
           A gipsy lad will come tonight.
           He will take you by the hand
           And lead you into gipsy land.

[*Looks in the mirror again.*] I'm sure they're gold. How would they suit me at a dance? The likes of me have only a hole like this to call our own, and a bit of broken mirror. But my lips are as red as madame's with her mirrors down to the floor and her fine gentlemen to kiss her hand. And I'm just a poor girl.

[*The child sits up.*]

Shush, child, shut your eyes. [*She flashes the mirror.*] There's the sand man running across the wall. Shut your eyes! If he looks into them you'll go blind.

[*Enter* WOYZECK, *behind her. She starts and puts her hands to her ears.*]

WOYZECK. What's that you've got?

MARIE. Nothing.

WOYZECK. There's something shining there. Between your fingers.

MARIE. I found an earring.

WOYZECK. Two at the same time? I never found anything like that.

MARIE. Am I a bad girl?

WOYZECK. It's all right, Marie. Look how he's sleeping. Hold his arm up, the chair's pinching him. He's got beads of sweat on his forehead. Nothing but work under the sun. Even in our sleep we sweat. We the poor. There's the money, Marie. My pay and something from the Captain.

MARIE. Bless you for it, Franz.

WOYZECK. I must be going. See you tonight, Marie.

[*Goes.*]

MARIE [*alone, after a pause*]. I'm a bad bitch. I could kill myself.—Oh, what's the use? We're all going to the devil, all of us.

Scene VII
At the DOCTOR'*s*.

WOYZECK, *the* DOCTOR.

DOCTOR. What a thing to see, Woyzeck. And you a man of your word!

WOYZECK. What's wrong, Doctor?

DOCTOR. I saw you, Woyzeck. Pissing in the street. Pissing up against the wall, like a dog. And me giving you threepence a day, plus board! That's bad of you, Woyzeck. The world is definitely going to the bad.

WOYZECK. But Doctor, when nature calls . . .

DOCTOR. Let it call! Haven't I proved that the *musculus constrictor vesicae* is subject to the will? Nature indeed. Man is free. Man is the transfiguration of the individual urge to freedom. Can't hold his water. [*Shakes his head, puts his hands behind his back and walks up and down.*] Have you eaten your peas, Woyzeck? Nothing but peas, *cruciferae*, remember. There's going to be a revolution in science, I'll blow the whole thing sky-high. Uric acid 0.10, ammonium hydrochlorate, hyperoxide.—Woyzeck, can't you have another piss? Go inside and try.

WOYZECK. I can't, sir.

DOCTOR [*upset*]. Pissing against a wall—and have I your written agreement! I saw it with my own eyes. I had just that moment put my nose out of the window to catch the rays of the sun—I wished to study the phenomenon of the sneeze. [*Going up to him.*] No, Woyzeck, I am not angry. Anger is unhealthy. Unscientific. I am perfectly calm. My pulse is its usual sixty and I say to you with the utmost sang-froid: God forbid that we should feel anger towards a fellow human being. Now if a newt had just died . . .! But Woyzeck, you shouldn't have pissed against that wall.

WOYZECK. But Doctor, some people are built that way. It's in their character. But nature's a different kettle of fish. As far as nature's concerned—[*He snaps his fingers.*] It's a kind of thing . . . I mean to say . . .

DOCTOR. Woyzeck, you're philosophizing again.

WOYZECK [*confidentially*]. Doctor, have you ever seen nature double? When the sun's at noon and it's like the whole world was going up in flames? That's when a terrible voice spoke to me.

DOCTOR. Woyzeck, you have an *aberratio*.

WOYZECK. It's all in the toadstools, Doctor. Have you ever noticed how the toadstools grow in patterns? If we could only read them!

DOCTOR. A classic case of *aberratio mentalis partialis* of the second order. Nicely developed too. I shall give you a rise, Woyzeck. Yes, second category: *idée fixe* but otherwise generally rational. Are you still going on as usual? Shaving the Captain?

WOYZECK. Yes sir.

DOCTOR. Eating your peas?

WOYZECK. Like you said, sir. The money goes to my wife for the housekeeping.

DOCTOR. Still carrying out your duties?

WOYZECK. Yes sir.

DOCTOR. You're an interesting case. Patient Woyzeck, you're getting a rise, so behave yourself. Let me feel your pulse. Yes.

SCENE VIII
MARIE's *bedroom*.

MARIE, DRUM MAJOR.

MARIE [*looking at him passionately*]. Show me how you walk. Broad as an ox and a beard like a lion. There's nobody like him. I'm the proudest woman alive.

DRUM MAJOR. By God, you should see me on Sundays with my plumed helmet and my white gloves. The Prince always says: That's what I call a man.

MARIE [*mocking*]. Does he now?　　　　　　　　　　[*Goes up to him.*]

DRUM MAJOR. And you're what I call a woman. Christ, we'll set up a stud for drum majors.

[*Puts his arms round her.*]

MARIE [*crossly*]. Let me go.

DRUM MAJOR. Wildcat.

MARIE [*violently*]. Don't touch me!

DRUM MAJOR. The very devil's in your eyes.

MARIE. Oh, what does it matter. It's all one.

SCENE IX
A street.

CAPTAIN, DOCTOR.

CAPTAIN [*comes panting down the street, stops and looks around*]. Doctor! Don't be in such a hurry. And don't wave your stick about like that. You're running to your death, you know. A good chap with a clear conscience doesn't rush about like that. Not a good chap. [*He catches the* DOCTOR *by the coat.*] Permit me to save a human life, Doctor.

DOCTOR. I'm in a hurry, Captain. In a hurry.

CAPTAIN. I'm so down in the mouth, Doctor. [*Emotionally*] I can't see my coat hanging on the wall but I burst into tears.

DOCTOR. Hm. Puffy. Fat. Thick neck. Subject to apoplexy. Yes, my dear Captain, you're heading for *apoplexia cerebri*. Of course you may only get it down one side. You may just be half paralysed. Or with a bit of luck it may only affect the brain. Then you'll live on like a sort of vegetable. That's your prognosis for the next four weeks. However, let me assure you that you're a most interesting case, and if the good lord decides to paralyse one side of your tongue we'll conduct experiments that will make our names go down in history.

CAPTAIN. Don't frighten me, Doctor. People have been known to die of fright, of sheer bloody fright. I can see the mourners already, squeezing lemons to make them cry. Still, they'll say: He was a good chap. A good chap. You damned old coffin-nail!

DOCTOR [*holding up his hat*]. Do you see this? This, my dear square-basher, is an empty headpiece.

CAPTAIN [*showing a button on his sleeve*]. And that, my dear coffin-nail, is a bonehead. Ha ha ha. No offence, Doctor, but I can give as good as I get. When I feel like it.

[WOYZECK *comes hurrying past.*]

What's the hurry, Woyzeck? Stop a bit. You rush through the world like an open razor. You'll give somebody a nasty cut. You'd think you had to shave a regiment of geldings and they were going to hang you with the last hair before you could make your getaway. But speaking of beards . . . What was I saying? Ah, yes. Speaking of beards, Woyzeck . . .

DOCTOR. Troops must be discouraged from wearing facial hair. Pliny says so.

CAPTAIN [*continues*]. Speaking of beards now, Woyzeck, haven't you noticed a hair in your soup lately? Do you follow? A hair from somebody else's beard—an engineer's, a sergeant's, or—a drum major's? Eh, Woyzeck? But then your wife's a decent girl. Not like the others.

WOYZECK. Yes sir. What do you mean, sir?

CAPTAIN. Look at the man's face! Perhaps not in your soup, but if you make a dash round the corner you may find one sticking to a certain pair of lips. Lips, Woyzeck. Ah, love—I know the feeling, Woyzeck.—Man, you're white as a sheet.

WOYZECK. I'm a poor man, Captain. She's all I've got in the world. If you're joking, Captain . . .

CAPTAIN. Joking? I joke with you?

DOCTOR. Your pulse, Woyzeck. Your pulse. Short, violent, skipping, irregular.

WOYZECK. Captain, the earth's as hot as hell. But I'm icy cold. Hell is cold, I'd bet on that. It can't be true. The bitch. It can't be.

CAPTAIN. Do you want a bullet through your head? And don't glare at me. It's all for your own good. You're a decent chap, Woyzeck, a decent chap.

DOCTOR. Facial muscles rigid, tense, occasionally twitching. Behaviour strained, excited.

WOYZECK. I'm going. A lot of things can be true. The bitch! Anything
can be true. A fine day, Captain. Look. A nice solid grey sky. Makes
you want to knock a nail in and hang yourself. All because of one
little train of thought. One that goes from Yes to Yes again, and
then to No. Is the No to blame for the Yes? Or the Yes for the No?
I must think about that.

[*He strides off, slowly at first, then faster and faster.*]

DOCTOR [*runs after him*]. What a case! Woyzeck, you're forgetting your
rise!

[*Exit.*]

CAPTAIN. Makes me quite dizzy, that chap. Look at him run. The
long-legged one loping like a spider's shadow. The little one jerking
along. The big fellow's lightning and the little one thunder. Grotesque, grotesque!

SCENE X
MARIE's *room.*

MARIE, WOYZECK.

WOYZECK [*stares at her, shaking his head*]. Hm. I can't see anything.
Can't see anything at all. You ought to be able to see it. You ought
to be able to hold it in your hands.

MARIE. What's wrong, Franz? You're raving.

WOYZECK. A sin like that. A great fat one. It stinks fit to smoke the
angels out of heaven. You've got red lips, Marie. And not a blister
on them. Marie, you're as lovely as sin. Can mortal sin be as lovely as
that?

MARIE. You're delirious.

WOYZECK. Damnation! Did he stand here, like this?

MARIE. It's a long day and the world is old. A lot of people can stand in
the same place, one after the other.

WOYZECK. I saw him.

MARIE. You can see a lot if you've got eyes in your head and aren't blind and the sun's shining.

WOYZECK. Bitch.   [*He makes to strike her.*]

MARIE. Don't touch me, Franz! I'd rather have a knife in my guts than have you lay a finger on me. My own father daren't touch me when I look at him, not since I was ten years old.

WOYZECK. Bitch.—No, it would show on you. Every man is a bottomless pit; you get dizzy when you look down. Suppose it were true. She walks like innocence itself. Well, innocence, there's a mark on you. But can I know for sure? Can anyone?

                                                    [*Exit.*]

SCENE XI
Guard room.

WOYZECK, ANDRES.

ANDRES [*sings*].   Mine host has got a pretty maid
                     Sits in the garden night and day;
                     She sits there in her garden . . .

WOYZECK. Andres.

ANDRES. Eh?

WOYZECK. Fine weather.

ANDRES. Sunny for Sunday. There's a band playing, out of town. The girls have gone on ahead. They don't half sweat.

WOYZECK [*restless*]. Dancing, Andres. They're dancing.

ANDRES. At the Horse and Stars.

WOYZECK. Dancing. Dancing.

ANDRES. Suits me.

  [*Sings*]   She sits there in her garden
                  Until the village clock strikes twelve,
                  Watching the redcoats passing.

WOYZECK. Andres, I can't sit still.

ANDRES. Fool.

WOYZECK. I've got to get out. My head's spinning. Dancing, dancing. Her hands will be hot. Damn her, Andres.

ANDRES. What's up with you?

WOYZECK. I've got to go. See for myself.

ANDRES. Trouble-maker. Because of that bitch?

WOYZECK. I've got to get out, it's so hot in here.

SCENE XII
A tavern. Open windows. Dancing. Benches outside.

APPRENTICES [, WOYZECK].

1 APPRENTICE [*sings*]. I've got a little shirt, but it isn't mine;
                    And my soul is stinking with brandywine . . .

2 APPRENTICE. Brother, let me knock you into the middle of next week. In a friendly way of course. Come on. I'm going to knock you into the middle of next week.—I'm as good a man as he is, see? I'll pole-axe every flea on his body.

1 APPRENTICE [*sings*]. My soul is stinking with brandywine.
—Even money rots. Little forget-me-not, what a lovely world we live in. I'm so sad I could weep buckets. I wish our noses were a brace of bottles. We could empty them down each other's throats.

OTHERS [*in a chorus*]. A hunter from the Rhine
                    Rode through the forest, oh so fine.
                    Tally ho, tally ho, as merrily we go,
                    Roaming the fields so free—
                    A hunter's life for me!

WOYZECK *goes over to the window.* MARIE *and the* DRUM MAJOR *dance past; they do not see him.*

WOYZECK. Him! Her! Damnation.

MARIE [*dancing past*]. On and on.

WOYZECK [*choking*]. On and on.

> [*Starts up, then falls back on to the bench.*]

On and on. [*Clapping his hands.*] Keep turning, round and round. Why don't you blow the sun out, God? Let them fall on each other in their lewdness. Male and female, man and beast. Do it in broad daylight. Do it on a man's hand like flies. The bitch is in heat. [*Jumps to his feet.*] Look at him pawing her, all over her body. He's got her, like I had her once.

> [*Falls back dazed.*]

I APPRENTICE [*standing on the table, preaching*]. Consider the wanderer who standeth and gazeth into the stream of time and answereth himself with the wisdom of God and saith: Wherefore is man? Verily, verily I say unto you: Wherewithal should the husbandman, the cooper, the shoemaker, the physician live, had God not created man? Wherewithal should the tailor live, had He not implanted shame in the human breast? Wherewithal the soldier, had He not armed him with the need for self-destruction? Therefore doubt ye not. . . . Oh, it's all very fine, but earthly things are evil. Even money rots. In conclusion, my beloved brethren, let's piss on the Cross and kill a Jew somewhere.

> [*General uproar.* WOYZECK *comes to his senses and rushes out.*]

SCENE XIII
Open country.

WOYZECK.

WOYZECK. On and on, on and on. Scrape and squeak—that's the fiddles and flutes. On and on.—Sh. Music. Who's speaking down there? [*Stretches himself full length on the ground.*] What's that you say? Louder, louder. Stab the she-wolf dead. Stab. The. She-Wolf. Dead. Must I? Do I hear it up there too? Is that the wind saying it? I keep on hearing it, on and on. Stab her dead. Dead.

SCENE XIV

A room in the barracks. Night.

ANDRES *and* WOYZECK *in the same bed.*

WOYZECK [*softly*]. Andres!

[ANDRES *mutters in his sleep.*]

[*Shakes him.*] Andres. Andres.

ANDRES. What's the matter?

WOYZECK. I can't sleep. When I shut my eyes everything spins round and I hear the fiddles. On and on. And then a voice comes out of the wall. Don't you hear anything?

ANDRES. Let them dance. A man gets tired. God save us, Amen.

WOYZECK. It keeps saying: Stab! stab! And flashes between my eyes like a knife.

ANDRES. Fool. Go to sleep.   [*He goes to sleep.*]

WOYZECK. On and on. On and on.

SCENE XV

Court-yard at the DOCTOR's.

STUDENTS *and* WOYZECK *below,* DOCTOR *at the attic window.*

DOCTOR. Gentlemen, here I am on the roof like David when he spied Bathsheba; but all I see are knickers on the line in the girls' boarding-school garden. Gentlemen, we come now to the important question of the relationship between subject and object. If we examine one of those creatures in which the divine spark achieves a high degree of organic expression, and if we investigate its relationship to space, the earth and the planetary universe—if, gentlemen, I throw this cat out of the window, what will be the instinctive behaviour of such a creature relative to its centre of gravity?—Woyzeck. [*He roars.*] Woyzeck!

WOYZECK [*catches the cat*]. Doctor, it bites!

DOCTOR. You fool, you're as gentle as if it were your own grandmother.

[*He comes down.*]

WOYZECK. Doctor, I'm all of a tremble.

DOCTOR [*delighted*]. Are you indeed! [*Rubs his hands, takes the cat.*] What's this, gentlemen? A new species of animal louse. And a very fine one.

[*Produces a magnifying glass. The cat runs away.*]

Animals have no scientific instincts. I'll show you something else instead. Observe. For three months this man has eaten nothing but peas. Note the effect, feel for yourselves. What an irregular pulse—and the eyes!

WOYZECK. Doctor, everything's gone dark.   [*Sits down.*]

DOCTOR. Cheer up, Woyzeck. A few more days and it'll all be over. Feel for yourselves, gentlemen.

[*They palpate his temples, wrists, and thorax.*]

By the way, Woyzeck, wiggle your ears for the young gentlemen. I meant to show you this before. He uses two muscles. Come on, man.

WOYZECK. Doctor—

DOCTOR. You clown, do I have to wiggle them for you? Are you going to behave like the cat? There you are, gentlemen; another case of progressive donkeyfication, a frequent result of feminine upbringing and the use of the German language. Your mother's been pulling out your hairs for souvenirs—it's getting quite thin these days. That's the peas, gentlemen. The peas.

SCENE XVI
The barracks square.

[WOYZECK, ANDRES.]

WOYZECK. Didn't you hear anything?

ANDRES. He's in there with one of his mates.

WOYZECK. He said something.

ANDRES. How do you know? What do you want me to say?—Oh he laughed and said: 'A luscious piece. What thighs! And she's hot as mustard.'

WOYZECK [*coldly*]. So he said that. What was it I dreamt about last night—a knife? People have stupid dreams.

ANDRES. Where are you off to?

WOYZECK. To fetch wine for my officer. But, Andres, there weren't many like her.

ANDRES. Like who?

WOYZECK. Never mind. Be seeing you.   [*Exit.*]

Scene XVII
A tavern.

DRUM MAJOR, WOYZECK, *people.*

DRUM MAJOR. I'm a man. [*Pounds his chest.*] A man, do you hear? Anybody looking for a fight? If you're not as pissed as creeping Jesus keep away from me. I'll ram your nose up your arse. I'll— I'll—[*To* WOYZECK] Hey, you. Drink up. Why isn't the world made of booze? Drink, will you!

[WOYZECK *whistles.*]

Bastard. Do you want me to yank your tongue out and wrap it round your waist?

[*They wrestle;* WOYZECK *is beaten.*]

I won't leave enough breath in you for an old woman's fart.

[WOYZECK *sits down on a bench, trembling and exhausted.*]

The bastard can whistle till he's blue in the face.

Brandy is the drink for me,
Brandy gives you spunk.

1 WOMAN. He's had it.

2 WOMAN. He's bleeding.

WOYZECK. One thing at a time.

SCENE XVIII
A pawn shop.

WOYZECK, *a* JEW.

WOYZECK. The gun's too dear.

JEW. You buy or you don't buy, which is it?

WOYZECK. How much is the knife?

JEW. Lovely and straight it is. You want to cut your throat with it?—
So what's the matter? I give it to you as cheap as anybody else. Cheap
you can have your death, but not for nothing. What's the matter?
You'll have your death all right, very economical.

WOYZECK. It'll cut more than bread.

JEW. Tuppence.

WOYZECK. There.   [*Exit.*]

JEW. There, he says. Like it was nothing at all. Well, it's all money.
Dog!

SCENE XIX
MARIE'S *room.*

[MARIE, *her child, the idiot* KARL *lying down, telling fairy-tales on
his fingers.*]

KARL. My lord the king has a golden crown. Tomorrow I shall bring
the queen her child, said Rumpelstiltzkin. Come, sausage, said the
black pudding.

MARIE [*turning the pages of the Bible*]. 'Nor was guile found in his mouth.'
Dear God, don't look at me. [*Turning further.*] 'And the scribes and
the Pharisees brought him a woman taken in adultery and set her in
the midst . . . And Jesus said unto her: Neither do I condemn thee.
Go, and sin no more.' [*Clasps her hands.*] Dear God, I can't. Almighty
God, at least give me strength to pray.

[*The child huddles against her.*]

The child breaks my heart. [*To the idiot.*] Karl!—He's basking in the sun.

> [KARL *takes the child and lies still.*]

No sign of Franz, yesterday or today. It's hot in here. [*She opens the window.*] 'And stood at his feet weeping, and began to wash his feet with tears, and did wipe them with the hairs of her head, and kissed his feet, and anointed them with ointment.' [*Beats her breast.*] Everything is dead. O Christ my Saviour, if only I could anoint Thy feet!

SCENE XX
Barracks.

ANDRES; WOYZECK *rummaging through his belongings.*

WOYZECK. Andres, this waistcoat isn't standard issue. You might find a use for it, Andres.

ANDRES [*numb, can find only a single word to say*]. Yes.

WOYZECK. The cross is my sister's, and so's the ring.

ANDRES. Yes.

WOYZECK. I've got a holy picture as well, with two hearts on it. It's real gold. Used to be in my mother's Bible. It says:

> Lord, as Thy side was red and sore,
> So let my heart be evermore.

My mother's got no feeling left, only when the sun shines on her hands. She won't miss it.

ANDRES. Yes.

WOYZECK [*pulls out a piece of paper*]. Friedrich Johann Franz Woyzeck, rifleman, Four Company, Second Battalion, Second Regiment. Born on the feast of the Annunciation, 20th July. I'm thirty years, seven months, and twelve days old today.

ANDRES. Go sick, Franz. You need *schnapps* with gunpowder in it. That'll lay your fever.

WOYZECK. Yes, Andres. When the carpenter puts his shavings in the coffin nobody knows whose head will lie on them.

SCENE XXI
A street.

MARIE *with* GIRLS, *at the front door*; GRANDMOTHER.

GIRLS [*sing*].   The sun shines bright at Candlemas,
                The corn stands full and high.
                Down in the meadow, two by two,
                They all came dancing by.
                The pipers led the way,
                The fiddlers followed after.
                They had red stockings on. . . .

1 GIRL. That's silly.

2 GIRL. You're never satisfied.

1 GIRL. Marie, sing for us.

MARIE. I can't.

1 GIRL. Why not?

MARIE. Because.

2 GIRL. Because why?

3 GIRL. Tell us a story, Granny.

GRANDMOTHER. Gather round then, small fry.—Once upon a time there was a poor little boy who had no father or mother. Everything was dead, and there was nobody left in the whole wide world. Everything was dead, and he went away and searched day and night. And because there was nobody left on earth he thought he'd go up to heaven. And the moon looked at him so kindly! But when he reached the moon he found it was a piece of rotten wood. And then he went to the sun, and when he reached the sun he found it was a withered sunflower. And when he came to the stars they were little golden gnats that a shrike had stuck on a blackthorn. And when he wanted to go back to earth, the earth was an upturned pot. And he was all alone. And he sat down and cried, and he's sitting there still, all alone.

[WOYZECK *appears.*]

WOYZECK. Marie!

MARIE [*startled*]. What is it?

WOYZECK. Let's go, Marie. It's time.

MARIE. Where?

WOYZECK. How should I know?

SCENE XXII
The edge of the wood, by the pond.

MARIE *and* WOYZECK.

MARIE. That must be the town over there. It's dark.

WOYZECK. You ought to stay. Come and sit down.

MARIE. But I have to go.

WOYZECK. You'd get sore feet; I won't let you.

MARIE. What's the matter with you?

WOYZECK. Do you know how long it's been, Marie?

MARIE. Two years come Whitsun.

WOYZECK. Do you know how long it's going to be?

MARIE. I must go and get supper ready!

WOYZECK. Do you feel cold, Marie? But you're warm, your lips are hot. Hot breath, harlot's breath. Yet I'd give heaven to kiss them again. Do you feel cold? When we *are* cold we don't feel it any more. You won't feel cold in the morning dew.

MARIE. What are you saying?

WOYZECK. Nothing.

[*Silence.*

MARIE. The moon's rising. Look how red it is.

WOYZECK. Like blood on iron.

MARIE. What are you going to do, Franz? You're so pale.

[*He raises the knife.*]

Stop, Franz, for God's sake. Help! Help!

WOYZECK [*stabs convulsively*]. Take that. And that. Why can't you die? There! There!—Still twitching; still can't die? Still? [*Stabs again.*] Now are you dead? Dead. Dead!

> [*He drops the knife and runs away.*]

> [MEN *come.*]

1 MAN. Stop.

2 MAN. Shhh. Do you hear? Out there.

1 MAN. Ugh. What a sound.

2 MAN. That's the water calling. It's a long time since anyone was drowned. Come away, it's not good to hear it.

1 MAN. Ugh, there it goes again. Like a dying man.

2 MAN. It's uncanny. Such a foggy day, with grey mist everywhere. And the beetles whirring like cracked bells. Let's go.

1 MAN. No, it's too distinct. And too loud. Come on, it's over there!

SCENE XXIII
The tavern.

[WOYZECK, KÄTHE, KARL, *others.*]

WOYZECK. Everybody dance. On and on. Sweat and stink. He'll get you all in the end.

[*Sings*]   My daughter, oh my daughter,
                What were you thinking of
                Hanging round grooms and coachmen
                And giving them your love?

> [*He dances.*]

Sit down, Käthe. I'm hot. Hot. [*Takes his jacket off.*] That's how things are: the devil takes one and lets the other go. You're hot, Käthe. Why's that? Be sensible; you'll catch cold. Can't you sing something?

KÄTHE [*sings*].   To the south land I'll not go.
                  I will not wear long dresses; no.

> For dresses long and pointed shoes
> A servant girl must never choose.

WOYZECK. No, no shoes. You can get to hell without shoes.

KÄTHE [*sings*].   Shame, shame, my love, the girl made moan:
Keep your money and sleep alone.

WOYZECK. I wouldn't want to get blood all over me. Honestly.

KÄTHE. What's that on your hand then?

WOYZECK. On me?

KÄTHE. You're all red. Blood!

[*People gather round.*]

WOYZECK. Blood? Blood?

LANDLORD. Ugh, blood.

WOYZECK. I think I cut myself. On the right hand.

LANDLORD. How did it get on your elbow?

WOYZECK. I wiped it off.

LANDLORD. What, wiped your right hand on your right elbow?
Genius, you are.

KARL. Then the giant said: Fee fie fo fum, I smell the blood of a
British man. Ugh it stinks.

WOYZECK. What the hell do you want? What's it to do with you?
Out of my way or the first man . . . Hell, do you think I've done
somebody in? Am I a murderer? What are you gaping at? Look at
yourselves. Out of my way.   [*He runs out.*]

SCENE XXIV
At the pond.

WOYZECK *alone.*

WOYZECK. The knife. Where's the knife? I left it here. It'll give me
away. Closer, closer. What sort of place is this? What's that noise?
Something's moving. Shh. Just over there. Marie? Marie! Nothing.

Not a sound. Why are you so pale, Marie? Why have you got that red string round your neck? Who did you sleep with for the necklace? Your sins were black. Did I whiten you again? Why is your hair so tossed—didn't you plait it today? The knife! Got it. There.

[*He goes to the waterside.*]

In you go. [*He throws the knife in.*] It sinks in the dark water like a stone.—No, it's too close, when they're bathing.

[*He wades into the pond and throws it further out.*]

There. But in summer, when they dive for mussels? Bah, it'll get rusty, nobody will recognize it. I wish I'd broken it. Is there still blood on me? I must wash it off. There's a spot. And there's another. . .

[*He wades in deeper.*]

APPENDIX

A Note on the Historical Woyzeck and Büchner's Design for the Play

The historical Woyzeck, according to the account of him by Dr J. C. A. Clarus, published in 1825 in the *Zeitschrift für die Staatsarzneikunde*, was a rolling stone who lost his parents early and wandered all over Germany looking for work in the difficult 1790s. He became a soldier, was captured by the Swedes, and entered the Swedish armed service, only to be sent back to Germany and have his regiment disbanded by the French. He then joined the Mecklenburg army, but deserted to the Swedes again because of a girl in Stralsund, by whom he had had a child out of wedlock. Then came the Congress of Vienna, which gave Swedish Pomerania to Prussia; Woyzeck's regiment was transferred *en bloc* to the Prussian army. This was not to Woyzeck's taste, so he asked for demobilization and returned to his native city of Leipzig in search of work. He was a hairdresser. Unfortunately times were hard, and Woyzeck became more and more dependent on other people's charity. He tried to enlist in the Saxon army but was turned down on the grounds that his demobilization papers were not in order. In the meantime he had formed a liaison with Frau Woost, the daughter of a surgeon; but she had a weakness for soldiers, and refused to appear in public with Woyzeck. In a fit of jealous despair he stabbed her, on 21 June 1821.

In character Woyzeck was not a criminal type. His intelligence was above average; he knew the trades of hairdressing and bookbinding. His main fault was drunkenness. He seems to have been driven to murder by a sense of humiliation built up over years of tribulation.

During the preliminary investigation of his case the defence claimed that Woyzeck was mentally disturbed; but Clarus, whom the court had appointed medical assessor, found him responsible. In February 1822 he was condemned to death by the sword. But then Woyzeck told a clergyman who visited him about his 'voices', and the defence demanded a stay of execution. A further medical examination was ordered. Clarus did not alter his judgement. He concluded that the voices did not pre-date Woyzeck's imprisonment, and were caused partly by his physical condition—his circulation was poor—partly by remorse, and partly by loneliness, which exaggerated his natural tendency to talk to himself. The defence asked to have Clarus replaced as assessor; but the Leipzig Faculty of Medicine upheld his opinion, and on 27 August 1824 Woyzeck was executed in the Market Square at Leipzig. He made a good end, facing death calmly and reciting a little prayer of his own composition which was later circulated as a broadsheet.

Long after Clarus published the account of his medical examination of Woyzeck, his findings were still being challenged; indeed the controversy over the case continued for thirteen years. The account shows Clarus to have been conscientious and fair-minded within his limitations, but sanctimonious and lacking that sympathetic understanding of human behaviour which Büchner brings to the story of Woyzeck.

Büchner left four separate manuscripts of the play, one that can with reasonable certainty be called the final version and three others. All are fragmentary and contain much overlapping material, yet we have Büchner's own word that he thought the play almost finished. In a letter to Minna a few weeks before his death he wrote, 'In a week at most I shall publish [erscheinen lassen] Leonce and Lena with two other dramas.' One of these two is presumably the already completed Pietro Aretino; the other is certainly Woyzeck, and Büchner's remark can only mean that he would have it ready for publication within the week. Unless there was a later, fifth manuscript (which I do not think is a justifiable assumption), we must believe that Büchner thought he could put what we now possess into order within that time.

Would that have been possible? Just about. When we look at the manuscripts we find that the 'final version' is fairly plain sailing up to the scene in which Woyzeck offers his belongings to Andres, after which it breaks off. But the order of scenes is puzzling. Woyzeck shaving the Captain, which many editors place at the beginning, comes fourth. And two scenes similar in tone—those where the Captain and the Doctor appear together—are placed beside each other. And there are gaps. Why? Büchner's own proceeding gives us a clue. After the scene in which Marie sees the drum major for the first time he simply writes

Booths. Lights. People.

and goes straight into the earrings scene. Clearly he felt that the fairground scenes were complete in the earlier version—and who, reading them, would disagree with that? So the 'final version' is really an extensive filling-in operation; and we need not feel too inhibited about assembling a definitive version of the play with the help of the earlier manuscripts—perhaps some of the added scenes were also finished to Büchner's satisfaction.

Various scholars have attempted the assembly job, with differing results. In 1879 Franzos deciphered the faded manuscripts and put together a more or less finished play from the various versions. Unfortunately, he made mistakes in transcription, the most obvious being in misreading the name of the principal character (which is why Berg's opera is called *Wozzeck*). In addition, to bring up the faded ink, he painted the manuscript with distilled water and sulphate of ammonia, which worked well at the time but as the years passed progressively blackened the paper. Later editors have corrected some of his mistakes and worked out different arrangements for the scenes. Fritz Bergemann (1922)—whose order I have for the most part followed in my translation—and Werner Lehmann (1967) are the most important. They differ in many respects. For example Lehmann starts with the Open Country scene, with Woyzeck and Andres cutting sticks; the shaving scene comes fifth, after the earrings. The most considerable of British Büchner scholars, Maurice Benn, rejected the ear-waggling scene in the belief that Büchner intended to replace it with the doctor reproaching Woyzeck for pissing in the street. Which of the various reconstructions one follows becomes a matter of personal choice: scholarship can do no more than establish probabilities as the manuscripts were left in so fragmentary a state.

I have adopted Bergemann's order because it makes good sense on the stage. But I have come to disagree with one of his decisions: placing the scene in which the two men arrive at the pond at the end of the play instead of immediately after the murder, where it would seem to belong: it is their arrival which makes Woyzeck run away.

Having completed the play in this way, however, we are left with some early manuscript material unaccounted for, of which the following short scenes are the most important:

(1)   CHILDREN.

1 CHILD. Let's go to Margret's.

2 CHILD. What's up?

1 CHILD. Haven't you heard? There's a dead body, a woman's. They've all gone to see.

2 CHILD. Where?

1 CHILD. To the left of the water meadow. In the little wood by the red cross.

2 CHILD. Come quick or they'll carry it in and we'll miss it.

(2)   *Idiot* [KARL], *child*, WOYZECK.

KARL [*holding the child on his lap*]. This little piggy went to market, this
    little piggy stayed at home.

WOYZECK. Boy. Christian.

KARL [*stares at him*]. This little piggy had roast beef.

        [WOYZECK *tries to fondle the child, but it turns away and screams.*]

WOYZECK. Oh God!

KARL. And this little piggy had none.

WOYZECK. Christian, I'll buy you a geegee. [*The child pushes him away*].
    There, there. [*To* KARL] Buy the kid a geegee.

                                            [KARL *stares at him.*]

WOYZECK. Giddyup, horsey. Giddyup.

KARL [*jubilant*]. Giddyup, horsey, Giddyup, Giddyup.

                                    [*Runs away with the child.*]

(3)   COURT USHER, BARBER, DOCTOR, JUDGE.

POLICEMAN. A good murder, a real lovely murder. You couldn't wish for
    a nicer job. We haven't had one like this for years.

The first two of these scenes are effective, and may easily be fitted into the
play, after the tavern scene where Woyzeck appears with blood on his
hands; I have not put them in because I think they are not strictly necessary
to the action. The third, obviously no more than a note, raises the
interesting question: did Büchner plan to write a trial scene?

I think it may well have been his original intention to write scenes
depicting both a trial and an execution. He had already done both very
successfully, in *Danton*. And he must have been strongly attracted by the
opportunities for social criticism they would have offered. But I believe
that he changed his mind. He left no sketches either of a court or an
execution scene, and to write one or both from scratch within a week, in
addition to all the other work to be done on the play, seems beyond even his
powers. In any case, even if brilliantly done, would not a court scene have
been an anticlimax after the bleak and terrible picture of Woyzeck wading
deeper and deeper into the pond?

ANTON CHEKHOV	Early Stories
	Five Plays
	The Princess and Other Stories
	The Russian Master and Other Stories
	The Steppe and Other Stories
	Twelve Plays
	Ward Number Six and Other Stories
FYODOR DOSTOEVSKY	Crime and Punishment
	Devils
	A Gentle Creature and Other Stories
	The Idiot
	The Karamazov Brothers
	Memoirs from the House of the Dead
	Notes from the Underground and The Gambler
NIKOLAI GOGOL	Dead Souls
	Plays and Petersburg Tales
ALEXANDER PUSHKIN	Eugene Onegin
	The Queen of Spades and Other Stories
LEO TOLSTOY	Anna Karenina
	The Kreutzer Sonata and Other Stories
	The Raid and Other Stories
	Resurrection
	War and Peace
IVAN TURGENEV	Fathers and Sons
	First Love and Other Stories
	A Month in the Country

GEORGE ELIOT	Daniel Deronda
	The Lifted Veil and Brother Jacob
	Middlemarch
	The Mill on the Floss
	Silas Marner
SUSAN FERRIER	Marriage
ELIZABETH GASKELL	Cranford
	The Life of Charlotte Brontë
	Mary Barton
	North and South
	Wives and Daughters
GEORGE GISSING	New Grub Street
	The Odd Woman
THOMAS HARDY	Far from the Madding Crowd
	Jude the Obscure
	The Mayor of Casterbridge
	The Return of the Native
	Tess of the d'Urbervilles
	The Woodlanders
WILLIAM HAZLITT	Selected Writings
JAMES HOGG	The Private Memoirs and Confessions of a Justified Sinner
JOHN KEATS	The Major Works
	Selected Letters
CHARLES MATURIN	Melmoth the Wanderer
WALTER SCOTT	The Antiquary
	Ivanhoe
	Rob Roy
MARY SHELLEY	Frankenstein
	The Last Man

ANN RADCLIFFE	The Italian
	The Mysteries of Udolpho
	The Romance of the Forest
	A Sicilian Romance
SAMUEL RICHARDSON	Pamela
FRANCES SHERIDAN	Memoirs of Miss Sidney Bidulph
RICHARD BRINSLEY SHERIDAN	The School for Scandal and Other Plays
TOBIAS SMOLLETT	The Adventures of Roderick Random
	The Expedition of Humphry Clinker
	Travels through France and Italy
LAURENCE STERNE	The Life and Opinions of Tristram Shandy, Gentleman
	A Sentimental Journey
JONATHAN SWIFT	Gulliver's Travels
	A Tale of a Tub and Other Works
HORACE WALPOLE	The Castle of Otranto
MARY WOLLSTONECRAFT	Mary and The Wrongs of Woman
	A Vindication of the Rights of Woman

The Oxford World's Classics Website

www.worldsclassics.co.uk

- Information about new titles
- Explore the full range of Oxford World's Classics
- Links to other literary sites and the main OUP webpage
- Imaginative competitions, with bookish prizes
- Peruse the Oxford World's Classics Magazine
- Articles by editors
- Extracts from Introductions
- A forum for discussion and feedback on the series
- Special information for teachers and lecturers

www.worldsclassics.co.uk

American Literature

British and Irish Literature

Children's Literature

Classics and Ancient Literature

Colonial Literature

Eastern Literature

European Literature

History

Medieval Literature

Oxford English Drama

Poetry

Philosophy

Politics

Religion

The Oxford Shakespeare

A complete list of Oxford Paperbacks, including Oxford World's Classics, Oxford Shakespeare, Oxford Drama, and Oxford Paperback Reference, is available in the UK from the Academic Division Publicity Department, Oxford University Press, Great Clarendon Street, Oxford OX2 6DP.

In the USA, complete lists are available from the Paperbacks Marketing Manager, Oxford University Press, 198 Madison Avenue, New York, NY 10016.

Oxford Paperbacks are available from all good bookshops. In case of difficulty, customers in the UK can order direct from Oxford University Press Bookshop, Freepost, 116 High Street, Oxford OX1 4BR, enclosing full payment. Please add 10 per cent of published price for postage and packing.